The Nones Are Alright

The Nones Are Alright

A New Generation of Believers, Seekers, and Those in Between

KAYA OAKES

ORBIS BOOKS

Maryknoll, New York 10545

ORBIS BOOKS
Maryknoll, New York 10545

Fathers and Brothers
MARYKNOLL™

Founded in 1970, Orbis Books endeavors to publish works that enlighten the mind, nourish the spirit, and challenge the conscience. The publishing arm of the Maryknoll Fathers and Brothers, Orbis seeks to explore the global dimensions of the Christian faith and mission, to invite dialogue with diverse cultures and religious traditions, and to serve the cause of reconciliation and peace. The books published reflect the views of their authors and do not represent the official position of the Maryknoll Society. To learn more about Maryknoll and Orbis Books, please visit our website at www.maryknollsociety.org.

Library of Congress Cataloging-in-Publication Data

Oakes, Kaya.
     The nones are alright : a new generation of believers, seekers, and those in between / Kaya Oakes.
          pages cm
     ISBN 978-1-62698-157-7 (pbk.)
     1. Church attendance. 2. Church membership. 3. Non-church-affiliated people. 4. Catholic Church. 5. Evangelicalism. I. Title.
BV652.5.O25 2015
277.3'083—dc23

                                                                                    2015013948

To my mother, sisters, and brother. Seekers all.

Contents

Acknowledgments

Thanks are due to Jim Keane for being both a great editor and a great writer, and to everyone at Orbis Books. Thanks to the people who helped with this book in its earliest stages, including Kerry Weber; Joe Hoover, SJ; Paddy Gilger, SJ; Mike Larkin; Heather Kirn-Lanier; and Charles Petro. Thanks are also due to my spiritual and theological advisers for patience with endless questions: Jean Sauntry, CSJ; Al Moser, CSP; Bernie Campbell, CSP; Bill Edens, CSP; Jason Welle, SJ; Aidan Putnam, OSB; Shay Kearns; Marissa Egerstrom; Greg Hillis; the women of my prayer group; and the ever-evolving group of writers, editors, theologians, clergy, seekers, doubters, and questioners on social media who provide guidance and support.

I owe special thanks to my Killing the Buddha colleagues for paving the way for writing about faith from the margins, with extra thanks to Nathan Schneider and Brook Wilensky-Lanford. Thanks also to my colleagues in the College Writing Program at U.C. Berkeley, to my students, and to the librarians at Berkeley and at the Graduate Theological Union. Ongoing gratitude goes out to the many writers I am also lucky to call friends, which would be a ridiculously long list, but special thanks to Sam and, as always, to everyone from Kitchen Sink. Thank you, Sage, for hanging in there with me. My deepest gratitude is owed to the many people I spoke to for this book, whether they are directly quoted or not. Your generous giving of time, your thoughtful responses, and your openness and honesty are invaluable.

Introduction

The Seekers

That I should give up my questioning was
good enough advice, which I would have
been glad enough to take, except that my
questioning would not give me up.
—WENDELL BERRY, *JAYBER CROW*

They started to appear on campus a few years ago. As an instructor at UC Berkeley I had long observed that we do a lot of things at Berkeley out in the open that would get you arrested or side-eyed anywhere else: nudity, dope, discussing Heidegger's concept of ontological change over falafels. We don't do naked emotion. But there they were: young, beautiful kids standing on Sproul Plaza, one of them playing a guitar, all of them singing with their eyes closed. And in front of them a sign, the all-caps words limned in gold: "God is IN LOVE with YOU."

I do not doubt that God is in love with these kids. Calling them kids is my first way of keeping my distance; none of them is my student. But I do spot one of my students soon after I walk through the resonating chords of the Jesus music they're keening as they sway and hug themselves. And my student is behind a table for the CRU, rebranded from its problematic former name, Campus Crusade for Christ. And at another table, Korean Christians for Christ, is another student. At every other table on the plaza students want to talk to you about Jesus. You would think the school had suddenly transformed from all that Berkeley entails into an evangelical school.

In Wheeler Hall, where my office sits half underground, I climb two flights of stairs and arrive winded, my arms full of papers and books and a laptop, at my creative nonfiction class. Today is draft day. The students want to write about pain and loss and death. "Those are kind of clichéd topics," I tell them, "but I'm not gonna stop you." And I read the drafts about pain and loss and death, and so many of them are about losing faith. Losing God and religion. One guy, so smart, tells the story of the day he no longer wanted to be Catholic, "because I want to scream at everyone in church that you're worshiping an implement of torture." I hand him back his draft with my careful comments; they say nothing at all about his newfound atheism but instead mention issues like sensory detail and first-person pronouns. The classroom is hot, and I sweat. So I open the window against protests from Southern California students who think anything under 70 degrees is freezing, kids who wear Ugg boots in summer, and one of them pulls his hoodie more tightly around himself, hugging himself, and in through the window it comes. The keening singing. The closed-eyes singing. Jesus. Jesus. Jesus is in love with me.

What I don't tell the students, or my friends, or my mother, or my siblings—what only my husband knows and isn't entirely happy about—is that on Wednesdays, a night when I should be at home resting up for the ten hours of teaching and meetings I have on Thursday, I sit in a room with sixteen people and talk about Jesus. Nobody closes their eyes, or hugs themselves, or sings. Nobody talks about God being in love with them. The priest reminds them that God loves them, yes, but there is no intimacy involved. We are Catholics, after all.

Here is what I wanted to write on that student's essay about leaving the Catholic Church. When I was nineteen, my father died. At his funeral mass I looked up at the cross and thought the same thing: I hate the pain I'm staring at. These people are worshiping pain. I know how you feel, I know it so well. The reason I did not write this: it is a public school. We don't talk about religion except in the context of books we read. We don't talk about our personal lives much at all, really, as it's not appropriate, even in a creative writing class, and at conferences and meetings we debate

this and the answer is always: No. Don't say it. Maybe the occasionally funny anecdote. We don't talk about prayer or faith or
the loss thereof, a loss that began for me when my father died and
continued for decades until I found myself back in a pew, back at
church, back in spite of everything I stand for: feminism, equality,
logic. And I prefer keeping this quiet, frankly, because my prayer
when I'm leaving the church, which is just blocks from campus,
when I'm walking with my head down, is please God don't let me
run into one of my students. Or one of my colleagues. Or anyone
I've ever met.

Faith is shame. It's the shame of seeing those closed-eyed evangelicals being enraptured by a God who knows them better than
any human could. It's the shame I feel at seeing Bernini's "Saint
Teresa in Ecstasy," a statue of such violently erotic and intimate
nature that, when I travel to Rome on a DIY pilgrimage, I'm
shocked to see it displayed in a church. Faith is the shame of Holy
Thursday, when everyone around me gets up to wash a stranger's
feet, and I am too paralyzed with hypochondria to move. Faith is
the shame of never doing enough: never volunteering as much as
those Catholic Workers who surrender everything for God, never
wanting to distribute the Eucharist at mass, never attending daily
mass but only showing up on Sundays and missing Sundays fairly
often, never praying before bedtime, never praying much at all,
never being as good as the nuns you see on the news boarding
a bus and confronting the government about its neglect of the
poor, never as good as the Franciscan who was the first to rush in
and the first body carried out of the World Trade Center on 9/11.
Those kinds of faith make you feel bad about yourself. Catholics
are very good at that.

Faith is being willing to stand on the steps where Mario Savio
stood and told us to throw our bodies on the gears of the machine,
and from there to sing about a rogue Palestinian Jew who stood
singing with the despised and marginalized and then threw his
body onto a primitive implement of torture in order to upend the
social order. But after I handed back that young atheist's essay,
two days later, in spite of my careful silence about the topic even
while I was preparing to be confirmed into the Catholic Church,

he dropped the class. I had met another Catholic woman who, like me, works for marriage equality and feminism and who has one foot in and one foot out of the church at all times, and she stood behind me at Easter as a priest slathered oil onto my forehead and the congregation sang "Veni, Sancti Spiritus," "Come, Holy Spirit," comforter, guest of the soul, consolation. And I wanted to find that young atheist and say, yes, you can walk away, and many of us walk away. But faith is a tidal motion, an ebb and a surge, a push and a pull.

Open eyes, closed eyes. Belief and disbelief. Between the emotive faith of those young evangelicals and the decisive self-severing of atheists from the possibilities of belief is a space of doubt and tension. It is where millions of Americans dwell. Anyone who was born after the 1960s has lived much of her or his life among at least some nonbelievers, doubters, and questioners. When the PEW Forum released the results of its multi-year study of religious life in 2012,[1] the news that up to one-third of people in their twenties, thirties, and forties describe themselves as having "no religion" was about as shocking as discovering that we really like iPhones. Of those between eighteen and twenty-nine, 31 percent describe themselves as "unaffiliated" with any religion; 20 percent of those between forty and forty-nine describe themselves in the same way. Among those unaffiliated people, however, the question of God's existence is less black and white than many would believe; nearly 60 percent of the unaffiliated are either "fairly certain" or "absolutely certain" that God exists, yet almost the same percentage believe that belonging to an organized religion is "not at all important." And it is not just Gen X and Millennial Catholics who are turning away from organized religion; in my social circle you can find lapsed Jews, lapsed Mainline Protestants, former evangelicals, ex-Muslims, kids raised Quaker, and even a former Buddhist monk. As a Bay Area native I may be running in a group of creative types who are more likely to eschew anything smacking of institutionalized thinking, but even my students (many of whom come from more conservative pockets of California, the

---

[1] PEW Forum, "Nones on the Rise," October 9, 2012.

United States, and deeply religious foreign countries) also reflect the PEW statistics. They are overwhelmingly disinterested in traditional notions of what it means to have faith. Instead of cleaving to one particular way of believing, many younger people engage in a kind of spiritual mix and match, blending many traditions and adhering strictly to none.

If faith is shame, faith is also struggle. There is no proof of God's existence; you may learn to recognize God, but it requires focus and time, two things most of us lack today. It can be difficult for younger people to find public witnesses to faith who are inspiring and integrity filled. And that struggle to believe without seeing is enough to push people of all ages away from the idea of God, or to push them into bending religion into something that better fits their individuality. We live in a time when technology enables faster and easier problem solving. Science breaks open mysteries and often resolves them. We want empirical evidence for everything, and we can usually find it without expending much effort beyond a Google search. Religion cannot hand us a God who appears in corporeal form. Religion tries to, but cannot explain away the horrors and fears of modern life. At its best religion can provide a deep and abiding sense of consolation, thicken our sense of compassion, give us community, and provide narrative and structure. At its worst it can be a vehicle to making us to feel judged and condemned, it can break up our families, exacerbate political tension, and deplete our inner resources.

Yet many of those who walk away from religion often do so with a sense of regret. Instead of becoming confirmed nonbelievers, they live in a space of permanent questioning. In a series of interviews with young nonbelievers on NPR entitled "Losing Our Religion"[2] a twenty-seven-year-old named Kyle Simpson talks about his agonized choice to abandon Christianity. Of his inability to believe in God he says, "I really want to. But there's nothing that clearly states 'Yes this is fact,' so I'm constantly struggling." He explains that science seems to clarify for him that God is an impossibility. But he still feels a desire to believe. "I think having

---

[2] NPR Morning Edition, "Losing Our Religion," January 15, 2013.

a God would create meaning for our lives," he continues. "Like we're working toward a purpose." Melissa Adelman, raised as a Catholic, echoes this: "Moving away from Catholicism for me was a loss, a negative thing, a rejection of a set of beliefs." But like many former believers, she argues that it didn't leave behind an "empty space." It created a space "you can fill with lots of really good things." Yet there is still a sense of loss; "tradition and community and support networks" were the things Catholicism provided for her that have subsequently been difficult to find in secular culture.

And it is perhaps that sense of tradition and community that keeps some atheist, borderline agnostic, or agnostic people in their faith traditions, even with all of their doubts. Even many vowed religious go to church deeply unsure why they're saying what they say. As a seminarian told me once, "We should just add 'maybe' to every line of the Apostle's Creed." A popular hymn tells us that "we walk by faith, and not by sight," which, when you think about it, means that many of us who are purportedly believers are ultimately walking around in the dark. Between doubt and the seemingly easier path of secularism it is easy to understand why people would choose to live without God.

My oldest friend, a guy I've known for nearly thirty years, is sitting across the table from me in a cramped Korean restaurant in Berkeley. We are both writers who come to the topic of faith from vastly different experiences. He's a lifelong atheist, raised by parents who blew off organized religion, someone who identifies with his distant Jewish roots but doesn't believe in God. Tonight we're talking about kids. He and his wife are beginning that conversation, and he wonders how religion will factor in. Talking about the Pledge of Allegiance as an example of how tough it might be for an atheist parent to deal with the prevalence of religion in schools, he says he hopes his kids will understand it's okay not to say that America is "one nation, under God."

"You know," my friend says, "it's just that I want to bring my kids up understanding it's okay to think there's no such thing as God."

Picking at the rice in my bibimbap, I nod. I love this guy like a brother, and I try to listen with compassion. But a nagging question bubbles up and spills out.

"If you bring up your kids with no God, what are you going to tell them to have faith in?"

My friend has a great depth of feeling. He's one of the few men I can adequately describe as a feminist. He's a listener. He respects what people have to say about religion, even if religion is not for him. So he listens to my question, the tinkling Korean pop music flooding the restaurant, and gives me the best answer he can.

"Well, I'm going to tell them that since there's no God, you have to have faith in other people."

Although I agree with the latter half of my friend's answer, I've also been having conversations like this with nonbelievers for most of my life. And those conversations have led me to realize that nonbelievers sometimes feel a sense of loss, but many of them still see the purpose of religion. Nonetheless, they don't feel obligated to commit to it. The media, however, has greeted the rise of the Nones with a mixture of "kids these days" and "their loss." In *When Spiritual But Not Religious Is Not Enough,* United Church of Christ minister Lillian Daniel uses barbed, snarky humor to try and convince nones that they just don't know what they're missing. In an interview with PBS she says "These people are always inform-ing you that they find God in the sunsets."[3] Adding another layer of irony to the icing on that cake, she goes on to say, "My take is that any idiot can find God in the sunset." Every time I read that line, it makes me cringe. I left my copy of Daniel's book on the table after skimming through it, and my agnostic husband picked it up and read bits and pieces. When I asked him what he thought of her approach, he replied that being mocked wasn't a particularly helpful way for a nonbeliever to find religion. If anything, Daniel's was the kind of approach guaranteed to keep him away from any church for good. "It'd be nice if someone treated nonbelief with, you know, compassion," he said.

---

[3] "Rev. Lillian Daniel on 'Spiritual But Not Religious,' *Religion and Ethics Newsweekly,* January 25, 2013.

When I try to explain to older religious friends whose children have left faith behind that this generational shift toward a kind of polyglot religion is not a reason for panic, even if it brings its share of sadness, my husband is one of the examples I hold up of why the nones are really all right. Raised by parents who themselves had grown up with very little religion, my husband has nonetheless maintained a lifelong curiosity about faith that has never manifested into anything more than curiosity. When we met sixteen years ago, I was firmly lapsed as a Catholic, and my stories of Catholic grammar school, replete with quirky nuns and salt of the earth priests, were mostly humorous to him. When I took an unexpected turn back into practicing Catholicism, his curiosity sometimes turned into suspicion that I might become right wing in a political sense. The public face of the church in America tends to look that way to an outsider. But I've held on to my left-of-the-left politics, and we've settled into a mutual respect for our differences. He's a working musician, and when we find that rare beast, a Catholic church with good music, he's happy to go, even if the experience includes taking a face full of holy water sprinkled by the priest. He is not a fan of the Paul Ryan, free-market philosophy-espousing types in Catholicism; neither am I. He admires the Nuns on the Bus; so do I. He finds the closest thing he can call God in music; so did Bach. So, for a time, did Bob Dylan.

Do I sometimes wish he'd wake up one day wanting to be Catholic? Sure. It can be lonely trekking to mass week after week without him, or without the company of one of my nonreligious friends. But I've forged my own community within Catholicism, one that can veer toward a kind of agnosticism. As progressive Catholics who sometimes feel left on the margins of faith, we talk a lot about why we stick with the church, for all of its obvious problems. And though I may be a believer, in many ways I'm still figuring out what I believe and why I believe it. That shrugging confusion, and a willingness to admit to it, makes faith less smug and more relatable to those on the outside.

In finding a way to be compassionate toward nonbelievers, it helps that many of my nonbelieving friends are not simply spending their Sunday mornings paging through the *New York Times* and brunching. They are actively engaged in community service and social justice issues. An atheist friend works in affordable housing issues in the African American community. Another atheist friend writes about feminist issues, particularly focusing on empowering young girls. The lapsed Catholic son of a friend travels to India to volunteer in medical clinics. A former evangelical I know works to bring attention to mental-health issues in the LBGTQ community. Atheist and agnostic students of mine have served in the Peace Corps, started food co-ops in inner-city food deserts, volunteered with literacy organizations, and taught inmates to read at San Quentin. No, most of them don't belong to an organized religion. But many are more compassionate, welcoming, and devoted to those on the margins of society than quite a few believers I know.

Lost in the hand-wringing over the rise of nonbelievers are these kinds of stories. And also lost are the stories of their own moments of doubt, confusion, fear, and even transcendence. In every conversation I've had with young nonbelievers, while some stories they tell of their loss of faith reflect a sense of sorrow, for many others, leaving one faith tradition behind to explore others, or to explore living without faith, has led to an amazing discovery. Outside of religious traditions that had told them they were sinful, told them they were damned, or told them they just weren't worthy of individual attention or time, they found freedom. They discovered their authentic selves. Some talk about returning to faith in the future. Others have checked out for good. But each of them is mature, self-aware, intelligent, and well informed. To leave religion was not a spontaneous decision. It was the product of discernment, thought, and yes, even of prayer.

The "restless heart" Saint Augustine described each of us having so long ago remains restless today. Even for committed believers in my generation the temptation to abandon organized religion is strong. Religion often fails to meet us where we arrive, hauling the complex baggage of modern life. And, perhaps, many young Americans are culturally moving into a way of being beyond organized religion. The Occupy movement, the Peace

Corps, Habitat for Humanity, and many other secular ways of living in community and doing service offer people the opportunity to engage in a form of life outside of institutionalized religion. Passionate, committed, and loving people want to meet other passionate, committed, and loving people, and oftentimes they don't meet them in church.

This is a challenge to what faith means today, perhaps even more so for my fellow Catholics. Why preach the gospel to a world that shrugs it off at every turn? Why bother with mass if God is present in the tents at the Occupy camp? Why tithe to Rome when Rome doesn't seem to know who you are or to care? Why bother with faith when faith brings us so much shame? If those who have left Catholicism and Christianity behind talk so much about finding fulfillment and joy outside of Christ, why bother with Christ? If week after week the couple next to you in the pew never says hello, why keep sitting there, feeling like an idiot for doing so? Is religion really just what the Catholic writer Fanny Howe calls "one more insane vision of the universe"?[4]

The answer, or at least part of it, is everywhere. The secular age. You can imagine it looming outside of church windows. Secularism doesn't bother me, most of the time, but when people around me hear a deeper call from God than my own, one that makes my calling within Catholicism as a writer and organizer seem shallow and weak, my own often wavering faith can begin to resemble a two-dimensional image. Many days it feels flat, and fake.

Within the last year three of my friends have moved more deeply into religious life, each following a very different path. One is a newly ordained Jesuit priest, one is in seminary for the Episcopal priesthood, and one is discerning his vocation as a Benedictine monk. Each of them has moved in and out of belief; each has in the past abandoned belief in God at one time or another. And yet enough of a nagging voice kept chasing them through the corridors of doubt, pursued them into a life of sacrifice and very hard work, and pushed them into taking the leap. Vocation gripped each of them and would not let go.

---

[4] "Fanny Howe Interview," *Bomb Magazine* (Winter 2013), 122.

As a married Catholic woman the door to a religious vocation was automatically shut to me and would never be open. Perhaps I didn't want it to be. But as these friends move on their paths toward ordination, and other friends and family members race away from religion as though their hair is on fire, and as religious friends rage over their wavering connections to faith or trudge to church without asking why they are trudging, for myself and many others, what it means to be between faith and faithlessness remains unclear.

The Franciscan Dan Horan points out that many people in the pews forget the fundamental thing about church: "If the assembly doesn't gather, there is no mass. And, if there is no mass, there is no church."[5] So just showing up? That's vocation. Because showing up is hard. And doing it week after week? Hard. And actually listening to the readings when you just got an iPhone, finally? Hard. But who acknowledges what that hardness means? And for all those beloved nonbelievers in my life, who among them ever asks how it feels to watch your generation turn its back on religion? I took this crisis to a spiritual director on a retreat, one of those absurdly named "busy person's retreat" (because who, in the modern world, is not busy?), where you check in for a few nights with a director without having to endure the narrow beds and bland food of a retreat house. After my book about my own journey out of and back into faith was published, I'd received a steady stream of messages from readers who had also left the Catholic Church behind, many of them asking for help in finding their way back. "But I have no vocation," I told the retreat director, a bearded young priest in a thick sweater and work boots. "I'm not a priest. How can I help these people?" He paused and then replied, "Do you remember what you were baptized as?" And I replied, "Well, my parents named me . . ." and he stopped me and said, "Listen: you were baptized as priest, prophet, and king. Well, queen. We've kind of forgotten this idea that the priesthood isn't just one guy."

---

[5] Dan Horan, "Giving Up Your Pew Is Not the Answer," *Dating God,* March 2, 2013.

However, the idea of embracing that collective priesthood proved elusive when the authority of the church intervened. Early in 2014 the newly appointed bishop of my diocese had, without explanation or warning, decided to remove two priests from the parish I'd attended since childhood. This parish has nourished and provided shelter for generations of skeptical and questioning Catholics, including my late father, my siblings, and myself. But when it came to losing two priests with no explanation, the congregation hardly felt like a body of priests. It felt vulnerable and confused. Although I had grown up in the era when news of a priest's removal was usually accompanied by agonized whispers about abuse, it was not the case here. Nor were we hemorrhaging parishioners or failing to attract younger ones. Nor had we spiraled into debt. Thus the news of the bishop's decision was met with distress and rage, and many parishioners walked, positive that this was a sign of worse things to come. As the months went by, the lack of explanation gnawed away at my belief in God. What I wanted were facts. What I got were evasions. A pew in a place that belonged to an institution that deliberately hurt so many people began to lose its appeal.

So it was from a liminal space, somewhere between faith and doubt, that I went looking for other doubters. In emails and messages sent to people I hoped to interview, I did not identify myself as Catholic, but as an agnostic Catholic, which made some people giggle, made others look puzzled, but made quite a few of them nod in recognition. In my travels and interviews I encountered atheist Jews, agnostic Christians, and even believers who, try as they might, could never pass from "I hope I have faith" into "I have faith." Perhaps we were loosely religious, but what we lacked was trust.

So I begin this book with a confession: sometimes I have faith, but far more often I have doubt. That puts me more in line with most of my peers, many of whom have absented themselves from organized religion, but who have not let go of the idea of God. Perhaps, as a generation, we are God bothered. Perhaps we were simply impatient, or bored, or, in my case, frustrated. Isolation kills the primary urge that draws people to religion, the urge to be part of a community. When that community shatters, isolation increases. When it fails to meet seekers where they come, bearing painful questions, they will turn away. When the community shuns them, they are gone.

But, as Wendell Berry's Jayber Crow puts it, "The questioning would not give me up." Who were my fellow travelers on the paths of doubt? Because I am a journalist and creative nonfiction writer rather than a theologian or academic scholar of religion, I didn't turn to books or conduct a survey; instead, I turned to people and used social media to expedite the search. In February 2014, I posted the following to my blog:

> The growth of the religiously unaffiliated young has sparked panicky debate in the pages of many newspapers and magazines. The rallying cry goes something like this: "What will they do without religion? How will they find a moral center? How can they engage in social justice without God? And how will religion survive without them?"
>
> As an agnostic-leaning believer, I want to prove those questions wrong. Very few people my age or younger are firm believers; most of us are seekers. That hasn't stopped us from fighting for greater social equality. It hasn't prevented us from reimagining faith as something we find in people rather than in institutions. And I'm beginning a book exploring the ways in which nones are really all right. But the book will also look at the ways people are reinventing what it means to "be church" outside of church walls, how people answer a vocational call in a time when religious vocations are down to a trickle, how people who don't "fit" in a particular religion nonetheless find ways to belong to it.
>
> So, I need you. I need to tell your story. Whether you grew up without religion, lost it, found it again, or find a unique way to belong to it, your story will help people to understand that faith exists and is in fact thriving in many surprising ways not always involving a "god." If you found faith in Occupy, in a queer community, in a social movement, in an intentional community; if you attend Sunday assemblies

or some other gathering for nonbelievers or prefer to go without faith on your own; if you stage underground communion services or are a heavily tattooed Orthodox Jew; if you're a feminist Catholic or an atheist who feeds people at a church soup kitchen—I want to know more. This project is about showing the world that there's no one way to believe and no one way to belong.

That blog post was forwarded to six hundred friends on Facebook and two thousand followers on Twitter, and was reblogged, shared, and re-Tweeted a few hundred times. Over the course of a year I conducted interviews in person, on Skype, and on the phone, each lasting about an hour, some lasting longer. Some of these subjects were people I already knew, but with whom I had never discussed religion and faith in depth. A few were friends of friends, but most were strangers. In several cases I followed up with people after our initial conversation; some of my subjects became regular correspondents with whom I exchanged emails, Tweets, and Facebook messages. In every case, instead of giving a snapshot of people's lives or positing theories based on survey data, I tried instead to tell the story of what led them to their current position as regards faith. My goal was to go deep rather than to go wide. If I really wanted to prove that the nones are all right, that meant getting to know them as individuals. So that is what I tried to do. In some cases names and identifying details of location and occupation have been changed. When I needed backup for a theory or a fact check, I did research, but for the most part I relied on my interviewees to speak for themselves instead of relying on surveys or statistics. And speak they did, often in ways that were thoughtful, eloquent, and challenging beyond my expectations.

Among those I interviewed, a large majority turned out to be, in one way or another, identified with Catholicism. This is perhaps unsurprising, given that one in every ten Americans is a lapsed Catholic. Were these people to start their own religious denomination, it would by some estimates be the third biggest one in America. Some were practicing but questioning their participation in the church; some had left the church for good; and some were "cultural" Catholics trying to make faith fit into lives that did not fit with what the institutional church says about sexuality and marriage. But the volume of people identified with Catholicism with whom I spoke meant that a large portion of this book would have to focus on that religion in particular, and how and why so many people have departed from it or found themselves marginalized by it.

Churches are, according to the religiously unaffiliated people surveyed by PEW, "too concerned with money and power, too focused on rules, and too involved in politics." Yet, a large majority also say that religion can "bring people together and strengthen community bonds." Do these people contradict themselves? Yes, they do. But what do we call the state between believing in God and the strength of community, but not wanting to belong to a religious community, deliberately choosing a life lived in liminal space? It seems that for many, that liminal space is beginning to look permanent, and as I discovered, it is even growing to absorb people who in the past might have wound up in religious life.

If even those called to a vocation are moving away from organized religion, what does that say about organized religion today? For younger people drawn to ordination, facing the complex questions of what ordination demands can be overwhelming. Chastity, poverty, and obedience have little to do with modern culture, and religious traditions that demand celibacy ask clergy to give up even more. Some congregations have shrunk so much that they cannot afford a full-time clergy member, meaning that clergy must split their time between multiple houses of worship or take up part-time jobs to survive. Seminary is expensive and time consuming, and a job in a desirable location—any job, in fact—is not guaranteed. Clerical life no longer garners the same automatic respect it once did. Some younger priests say that when they travel, they prefer not to wear clerical garb, because they're looked at with suspicion instead of respect. Family members can sometimes react to the news of a vocational call with distress instead of celebration. As a result of all of these factors, many people who would prove to be capable leaders for these new generations of doubters, seekers, and uneasy believers abandon the idea of a traditional vocation. They care deeply about religion but are unable to fit into what it expects of its clergy. Or they are ineligible for reasons of gender or sexual orientation to become clergy in the first place and must channel that vocation into other ways of life. Unlike the stereotypes about the religiously unaffiliated, these people are not apathetic; they care deeply about religion. Yet it has become difficult for them to negotiate what it means to answer a vocational call in a time when the call itself leads to a series of questions rather than a set of answers.

What was clear even from my own position of drifting to the edges of faith was that instead of looking at the believers and the nonbelievers around me and trying to understand how they'd wound up where they were solely based on observation, I needed to be with them. To ask questions. To tell stories. To engage. I needed to find out where those who'd left religion had gone, where they were going, to discover why people stayed in the church, to find out what it means to "be church" outside of church, to discover if people can "be church" without God. If nonbelief is freedom, what does it mean to have belief? Was every one of us really, deep down, just a seeker? "Ask and you will receive, seek and you will find": what? Somewhere in between the rejection of God by the committed atheist, the questioning of God by the wavering agnostic, and the trust in God of the true believer, there were millions of people who lived, every day, on the edge of doubt. On the edge of faith. Most of my life had been lived on the margins. So that's where I went: to the margins of religion, and to the margins beyond. To the singing "Jesus-y" kids on Sproul Plaza, to the atheist kids fleeing the church, to the people who stood in between. I went to the seekers, to see what we would find.

1

Nothing from Nothing

The many people I spoke to over the course of a year ranged from those teetering on the edges of institutional religions to those embracing a full-blown rejection of all religion. But atheists, often the loudest voices to speak against religion in the media, were in the minority of those who responded to my queries. I'd expected that atheists would appear en masse, but self-described atheists make up only about 2.4 percent of those surveyed by PEW.[1] In fact, more people describe themselves as not believing in God or a "universal spirit" than describe themselves as atheists. Whether fewer atheists responded to my queries because atheists choose not to align themselves with Nones, who more often describe themselves as unaffiliated believers, or because my background as a writer about religion was off-putting to a few of the atheists I contacted, I spoke to only a handful of people who were willing to categorize themselves as atheists. In each case, however, those atheists admitted that atheism today has a public image problem.

In *Faitheist*, writer and Yale humanist Chaplain Chris Steadman moves from childhood in a nonreligious family to a conversion to Christianity in a moment of teenage fervor, and then to an abandonment of religion when he questions its view of him as a gay man. But unlike many of the more well-known celebrity atheists, Steadman does not go so far as to reject religion completely. He even attended seminary and worked for years with Eboo Patel's

---

[1] Michael Lipka, "Five Facts about Atheists," Pew Research Center, October 23, 2013, http://www.pewresearch.org.

Interfaith Youth Corps. He chose to work side by side with the religious as an atheist rather than dissociating himself from religious people altogether.

Steadman describes the shock he received when he attended an atheist conference and discovered that it "was packed full of blasphemy sessions and speeches comparing religion to sexually transmitted diseases."[2] Upon calling another atheist friend and reporting his disgust with the tone of the conference, Steadman's friend said, "This is why I don't want to call myself an atheist." Steadman quotes Reza Aslan, who pinpoints the problem with the public face of atheism in a column for the *Washington Post.* Aslan writes, "It is no exaggeration to describe the movement popularized by the likes of Richard Dawkins, Daniel Dannett, Sam Harris, and Christopher Hitchens as a new and particularly zealous form of fundamentalism—an atheist fundamentalism."[3] Steadman agrees with Aslan's point that "the loudest voices are the most obvious," but he also argues that atheism's emphasis on critical thinking is what keeps it from tipping over into something resembling fundamentalism.

Steadman's book provides a different exposure to atheism from the books by Dawkins and Hitchens. Their sneering and condescending attitude toward even the most tentative and marginalized believers was tough to take; in particular, Dawkins's increasingly abrasive public persona was off-putting to the extreme. On July 27, 2014, for example, he stated on Twitter, "I hate the hereditary mental illness called religion." This may have garnered Dawkins a loyal following, but it also smacks of the kind of fundamentalism that Aslan refers to. So my expectations of atheists were pleasantly upset by Steadman's book, which calls for a much more tolerant, open-minded sort of atheism, one that doesn't exist separately from the lives of the religious but, rather, alongside them.

My skepticism about atheists being abrasive and unfeeling was further squashed when I sat down to talk with an atheist I'd known

---

[2] Chris Steadman, *Faitheist* (Boston: Beacon Press, 2012), 145.

[3] Reza Aslan, "Harris, Hitchens, Dawkins, Dennett: Evangelical Atheists?" *Washington Post*, July 16, 2010.

for nearly thirty years. Sam was one of the first people to respond to the blog post I wrote. His email was to the point: "About the atheist thing, I'm here whenever you need me."

I'm not sure at what point it was in our friendship that I realized that Sam was an atheist. My career in Catholic school was ending when we met at the age of fourteen; I'd been struggling at the all-girls Catholic school my sisters had also attended and was on my way to transferring into an alternative high school. Sam went to the big public high school in Berkeley, and at some point we must have talked about religion. We were both the sort of adolescents who get into long, deep conversations about life, and religion probably hovered somewhere in those discussions. We still talk about religion now, just as we still talk about literature; we're both journalists, so our discussions of faith tend to tip into the political and social rather than the personal. But, over coffee on an April afternoon, Sam was happy to crack open what it meant to be a lifelong atheist raised in a household with no organized religion. As it turned out, he was not only an atheist but he was a third-generation atheist.

Sam's childhood experience of religion was defined by the fact that both of his parents are nonbelievers. During his childhood, his mother sang in the choir at San Francisco's counter-cultural Glide Memorial Church, but she wasn't clear about what her religion was. Of church, Sam says, "I went sometimes, but sermons were less about God stuff. It wasn't pushed, and I didn't pay attention." However, his father's lack of attachment to organized religion was much clearer. "Dad is an atheist," he says. His father comes from an atheistic family as well: Sam's paternal grandmother was "anti-religion. Dad is interested in religion," he reflects, "but he looks down on it." Like a Catholic family that moves from practicing Catholic grandparents to Easter and Christmas parents to non-practicing kids, atheism softened through generations in Sam's father's family. Unlike the more strident atheism of his grandmother and father, Sam's atheism is of a new sort, one that lets believers be.

Sam's parents divorced when he was five years old, but for the sake of Sam and his younger sister, they continued to celebrate

Christmas together, with Sam's dad staying over the night before
to wake up with the kids in the morning. Of his father's atheism,
Sam says that it "wasn't a real big thing. Not believing in Santa
was more upsetting. When I was seven I found the Christmas
paper in the attic." The family's other nod to religion was the occasional Passover Seder held to honor the memory of Sam's paternal
grandfather, a ritual that Sam liked "because it involved food." But
beyond those gestures toward tradition, "it wasn't drilled into me
that they didn't believe."

At some point when Sam was attending grade school, he had
a conversation with his father about the Pledge of Allegiance and
made the decision to stop saying the "under God" part. Throughout his childhood he developed a growing interest in mythology: Greek, Arthurian, and comic book mythology that, he says,
"played a role in the absence of scripture." Even at a young age,
however, he was developing a highly critical lens: "When I was a
kid I was concerned about canon. Contradictions in Greek myths
were frustrating. The same thing happened in comic books." Years
later, Sam wrote a play based on Helen of Troy, and he is now
at work on a memoir based on "heroic stories of choice" that he
absorbed from comic books. But Sam's nonbelieving childhood
would lead him into more critical examinations of religion and
faith as he grew into a teenager and college student.

In high school Sam had "fascinations with . . . history and pag-
eantry and Antipopes and schisms." The fact that he was an atheist
didn't really matter at Berkeley High. As he puts it, "Nobody I'm
close to has ever tried to convert me. In a way I've been privileged
and sheltered in the Bay Area. It's not an issue here with people
trying to convert you. So it's been easy for me to be an atheist."
In fact, the parallel I experienced at a small alternative high school
right up the street from Sam's was that coming from a Catholic
family, I was considered to be the weirdo. Most of my classmates
self-identified either as nonbelievers or as some mishmash of
Buddhism and other Eastern traditions picked up by their Boomer
parents and passed on to the kids. The only openly religious kid at
my high school was Jewish, but his father was a rabbi who'd been
a member of the Seattle Seven and who later started a magazine

of progressive Judaism. Berkeley was a perfectly fine place to grow up if you came from a family like Sam's or if your religious practice was a mishmash.

When it came time to attend college at San Francisco State, Sam briefly toyed with studying psychology. He'd long known he wanted to be a writer, "but didn't consider it an occupation— I didn't want to be molded into a certain kind of writer." What drew him, instead, were the things that made people think the way they did, the "underlying philosophical assumptions . . . the ways people saw the world and accounted for human experience." So the atheist from Berkeley wound up double-majoring in philosophy and religion. Religion courses at SF State were "more focused on the inner mystical tradition versus orthodox traditions" and blended study of Western and Eastern religion together. Most were taught by the religious scholar Jacob Needleman, who had coined the term *New Religious Movements* in the 1970s to describe the new faiths rising out of the Boomers' experimental lifestyles. Sam's lifelong curiosity was the perfect fuel for looking at how religion and thinking intertwined from the point of view of a person standing on the outside of the religious traditions he was studying. "It was clear I wasn't going in as a seeker," he says. "I didn't have big questions. Because I never had religion, I wasn't rebelling against it." However, certain texts deeply resonated with him, particularly the existentialist thinking of Jean Paul Sartre and Simone de Beauvoir, who he interpreted as calling for readers to "be responsible for your choices."

At the same time, Sam began spending time at the Berkeley collective household Greyhaven, which fantasy writer Marion Zimmer Bradley described in 1983 as "an extended family, a state of mind." Two of Zimmer Bradley's brothers were also writers, and one of those brothers married another writer, and "a large number of people passing through turned out also to be aspiring writers, who were given houseroom."[4] Most of the younger people who hung

---

[4] Marion Zimmer Bradley, "Greyhaven: History of a Household," http://www.grendelheim.com.

out around Greyhaven were around Sam's age, in their late teens and early twenties, and were also "second-generation Pagans"; the original members of the household not only wrote fantasy novels but studied and practiced Pagan religious traditions and passed them on to their kids. One of the original Greyhaven residents founded the Society for Creative Anachronism, a group of people who get together to reenact the Middle Ages, including forays into practicing pre-Christian religions. Greyhaven hosted Pagan study groups and a Pagan Kabbalah class that Sam participated in, during which he had a "semi-mystical experience." But, he continues, "I saw it as a metaphor. I found it powerful without believing in it. I dabbled in these things without ever losing the atheist identity."

Sam graduated from college and spent time traveling around Europe, eventually winding up in Budapest, where he stayed for several months; several years later, after working at an alternative weekly newspaper in the Bay Area, he returned to Budapest again, where he wrote for an English-language newspaper. It was in Hungary that "encountering anti-Semitism for the first time made me consider my Jewish side." Sam's paternal grandfather was Jewish, meaning that Sam is "technically not Jewish." But "living in Hungary and encountering that brutality and those anti-Semitic beliefs . . . galvanized me." He realized that anti-Semitists of the kind he encountered in Hungary wouldn't bother to research his family tree, and that knowledge caused him to begin considering what it meant to be a person of Jewish ancestry, if not a practicing Jew. "It's an ethnic pride thing," he says. "I flirted with converting [to Judaism] for a while but was uncomfortable with the in-between-ness."

His marriage further pushed him into considering his relationship to religion, because his wife is a religious studies scholar who practices Hinduism. "The willingness to experience these things," different religious traditions, "has become important in my marriage. But I don't get swept up." At the wedding the couple combined rituals and symbols from Judaism and Hinduism, even calling it their "HinJew" wedding. Of his wife's view of his non-belief, Sam says, "She thinks of me as a spiritual atheist, but she's in a [religious] tradition where there are ceremonies and levels of initiation that married couples usually go through together. I wasn't interested but was willing to go along—but it'd be bare minimum." Over the ensuing years they've established a respectful appreciation for their religious differences.

However, no matter how comfortable he is inwardly with atheism, Sam struggles with the public perceptions of atheists. "It remains frustrating that atheism is equated with anti-religion. But I'm not opposed to a belief in God." It's only in the face of proselytizing that he becomes "crotchety about it because of people being pushy about religion—it makes me want to push back." The noted spokespeople for atheism, often so vicious in their attacks on religion, don't represent where Sam stands in his relationships with believers. "Dawkins and so on I find obnoxious and condescending," he says. "I don't feel superior to believers. I'm frustrated by dogma but don't feel superior. But I don't want an atheist community; it's ultimately not relevant. As long as belief doesn't come between us it's not a problem."

Ultimately, Sam acknowledges how important it was to becoming a more tolerant sort of atheist that he grew up in a place where religion was not a prominent issue. "I think it's important that my experience would have been different growing up somewhere else," he says. "If I'd had something to react against. Like more pressure in school." He reminds me of this as we push our coffee cups onto a bus tray and shoulder our bags on the way out the door. Berkeley was a gift to Sam's growth as a nonbeliever. "I had the luxury," he says, "not to push back."

Mark, a musician and art director at an advertising agency, grew up with only vague ties to religion. He was raised primarily by his mother and grandmother, who belonged to Jones Methodist Church, a Black Methodist church in San Francisco's Japantown neighborhood. Japantown overlaps San Francisco's Fillmore district, which was the historical home to many of the city's African American families. Mark's grandmother, now in her early nineties, arrived in San Francisco during World War II and was a fairly regular churchgoer. His mother, however, "only went to church occasionally." She rarely took Mark along; he remembers going "to an Easter service at age twelve and thinking, this goes on all day?" Today, he says: "Religion is Mom's hobby. She enjoys reading about it. It's an interest." But religion remained an abstract concept for much of Mark's early life.

At one point in his childhood Mark attended a Lutheran day school. "I didn't know what Lutheran meant for a year. One day, they played a 1950s movie about Martin Luther, and he was beating himself and nailing things to a door." Lutheranism, he says, was treated "like PE"; it was part of the curriculum, but more of an elective than a required course. At home "we had bibles," which gave him a few rudimentary tools to work with when it came to talking about religion. "I knew the stories. That probably helps in America."

"The biggest awakening was in college," he says. Mark enrolled in college at the age of sixteen, as one of the very few black students in the elite engineering program at UC Berkeley. "Because I went to college at sixteen," he says, "I knew nothing. I liked college and the atmosphere." But, he says, he "didn't really care" about college, and "only African drumming and world religion classes made me care." Mark's first exposure to religious studies made him realize that "religion is real. The psychology of religion, given choices about worship, people made decisions that meant a lot to them."

The discovery of what religion meant to others led Mark to a pivot point in his life as a student. Like the people he was studying who pursued religious vocations, "I wanted to do something that meant a lot to me." He talks about understanding religion for the first time as a revelation about how much he "didn't know," but also as a point at which it became clear that he was beginning to feel stifled by college and might need to create an alternate path for himself. "I didn't want to start a religion, but I didn't love being an engineer." It was in the religious studies course that Mark learned that Freddie Mercury, the late singer from the band Queen, had been born into a Zoroastrian family in Zanzibar and had first been exposed to music through religion. For Mark, this seemed to be a sign. Music, he realized, could also be a calling.

Mark dropped out of college to pursue music in earnest. He'd begun writing songs when he was ten years old and played the guitar "every day from twelve to sixteen." His parents, he says, "were completely against the music thing" and very unhappy about his decision to quit school. But Mark and two friends (full disclosure: my husband was one of those friends) formed a band called Endangered Species and "spent four years just writing songs while working [menial] jobs. It was great. I realized how little I knew, so staying at school was like *The Matrix*—after you take the pill, you're done."

When it comes to the overlap between music and religion, Mark says that at some point in his childhood "I got interested in magic. How do cups and balls and rings work? Mom got me a magician trainer. What you realize is that it's a trick. You fool someone's senses; people are happy. If you turn levers, you get a response. It's the same thing being in a band. People respond." Mark describes the work of being a musician as "getting people to think things. So my reaction to religion is that if you believe most people are decent, fearful, and have awe, starting a religion is a great gig. Music is the same. So the desire to be in religion is based on what most people want. Why watch fireworks? Why go see bands in a club? People are in search of awe and awesomeness."

Mark's lifelong disinterest in joining a religion, he says, has more to do with his personality than anything else. His summary of that is "I'm not a joiner." When he moved into a career in advertising, he learned that he preferred "when I can pick the team at work. People in religion don't mind group dynamics so much." Part of this resistance is a deep-seated sense that he swims upstream. "I'm too iconoclastic to get the nature of groups. I like community, but under every community are tribal beliefs. I like to be around people who will tell me no." When it comes to belonging to a religion, that feels like the antithesis of what works for him. He has no interest "in going to a building once a week, listening to someone talk, and giving money. But," he adds, "I live in a metropolitan area. It's not like I'm a white guy from the Midwest. My community is Facebook, people who listen to music. Don't know if it'd be stronger if we all believed in the same deity."

Mark and his wife, who "didn't really grow up in religion either," have three young sons. When I ask if the kids have started asking questions about religion or God, he says that hasn't really been the case. "They're aware of religion. Their first Bat Mitzvah was my first one." However, "they're not particularly interested either way. They know blond Jesus isn't accurate. They know there are different religions. But none of their close friends are religious, or they haven't shared that." Growing up in the culturally and ethnically diverse city of Oakland, Mark's kids "have a lot of Jewish friends and first-generation Asian and Indian friends. They see the multiplicity of religions." Mark says that if he asked his kids, "they'd probably say there's a God." But for his family, that's as far as it goes.

For all of Mark's iconoclasm, however, he admits that he finds surprises in learning about religion. He's intrigued by Jewish ideas about the afterlife. He also admits that he finds Mormonism "fascinating. It works for them. Sometimes I feel like religions are political parties. At some point you can't buy in. With Mormons that was when they wouldn't allow black people in." But, he says, at some level, religion is cultural, and part of who he is and his family's history, even while he chooses not to participate in it. "I do love fiery black preachers and old women in hats who do call and response."

Katie, who is in her thirties and studying for a PhD, also grew up in a nonbelieving family. Katie is biracial: half Chinese American and half white. Of her mother's Chinese American family in California, she says, "I was never aware that religion existed at all. There was no conversation about religion or spirituality whatsoever. Just nothing." Her father's family lived in rural Washington State, and her paternal grandparents were at some point churchgoers, "but by the time I was old enough to pay attention they were kind of over it." At one point in her childhood Katie exclaimed, "Oh, my God!" and her paternal grandmother told her not to say that, but, as she puts it now with a laugh, "I didn't have a reference point for understanding what was wrong with that."

It wasn't until she was seventeen and nearly out of high school that Katie had "a best friend who became a boyfriend," whose father was a Lutheran pastor. "That was probably the first time I ever went into a church, definitely the first time I heard anybody talk seriously about religion or God. I barely retained any of it, because it seemed like a fairy tale." Friction began to arise between Katie and her boyfriend's family, who perceived her as "pulling their son from the church," which was incorrect; her boyfriend was a punk rocker and not that interested in religion himself. However, Katie wound up spending a summer working as a counselor at a camp run by her boyfriend's father. "I believed in the community," she says, but at the camp, where she was supposed to be teaching Bible lessons and songs, she admits that "I was an abject failure at that, and had a lot of explosive arguments with other counselors." Throughout every argument with her boyfriend's father about Christianity's history in global warfare and her own pacifism, they remained at loggerheads. "It was an oil and water situation. It was my first experience of dealing with church community, and it went pretty poorly."

Religion didn't intrude much on Katie's undergraduate years at a public university. However, she worked at a bookstore during that time, where she did interact with religious customers: "I could tell which religion because of the books they were buying and how they talked to me," she says. There she discovered that a large chunk of spiritual seekers on the West Coast have something in common. "The takeaway" about religion from her bookstore years "was that there was a huge group of angry people trying to get into Zen Buddhism." Katie says she saw the angry would-be Buddhists as pursuing a "religious trend" and describes the experience as "seeing the way American society was using Buddhism, and it was hypocritical. They had bad attitudes and were looking for books about peace."

Katie has also studied yoga for some years, and again, she runs into the occasional spiritual seeker chasing Eastern religion but not really trying to understand it. She has "come into contact with mainly white women who practice yoga and have some adherence to what they'd call yogis or Hindu beliefs. I take that with a grain of salt." She describes yoga as a practice that brings her "some peace," but she doesn't hang that on Hinduism, the root religion of yogic practice, and finds it troubling when "privileged Americans become the proponents of those beliefs. Without context it becomes very self-serving." For example, there's a lot of chanting in yoga classes, and, Katie says, most of the people doing the chanting have no idea what it means. "To me, it seems very much like they're tourists," she says. "Taking on a tradition without thinking about how it arose."

Rather than seeking a religious path of her own, Katie finds two sources for the kind of fulfillment many believers gain from church attendance. Her father was "wary of people and more comfortable in nature," and he passed on to her a love and appreciation of the outdoors. "At one point," she says, "I was frustrated and broke, and said to my dad that I was sick of living in the city. I needed to get away and live alone in Western Montana or something. And he said, 'You're not really alone out there; there's thousands of deer and elk.' That encapsulated his spirituality: minimal, but on the same plain as any other living being." Katie took this creed with her into her adult life. "Being outdoors, my class and ethnicity don't matter. That's where I experience a spiritual relationship. It's very nonhuman. It's about being as tiny as any other thing on earth. That's very powerful and liberating but tends to push me away from any organized religion, where who you are and how you interact become more important."

Her other passionate engagement comes from community organizing and activism, but, she says, "I do that in an extremely secular way. A lot of community organizing can be proselytizing. I do more of the grassroots kind of organizing where there's not such a hierarchy in the structure." In the city where her university is located, Katie is engaged in anti-capitalist collective work, including a childcare co-op, staging weekly dinners, and providing a place for the unemployed to gather. She describes herself politically as "kind of an anarchist," but not a Black Bloc sort of anarchist (the anarchists who started trouble at many of the Occupy sites), but instead trying to break down structures of authority in order to enable greater self-responsibility in individuals. She's also part of a feminist collective, where the decision-making process is not hierarchical but instead requires "full participation from everybody. Talking and building with people about undoing oppression." She admits that this kind of process-based decision making is difficult and takes a long time, because "in mainstream American culture people are really taught not to work collectively or explain their decisions. They're taught to be not patient."

Katie notes that "there actually is really strong community in many churches" near where she is studying. However, her collective's attempts to work with the local churches has so far been unsuccessful for a variety of reasons, but primarily because of the issue she mentioned earlier about hierarchical decision making in church communities. As she puts it, "It's not natural [for churches] to have this totally horizontal approach to things." Her feminist collective has experienced some friction as well with the "really strong Italian Catholic" culture. Because the local culture is "more puritanical," she says, when she began studies "it was imperative to find likeminded people and try to grow that group of people." Community became more and more important to her as she got older. Growing up in the Bay Area, there "was a feeling that everybody was involved in some movement, some social justice kind of thing. Here you have to look deeper for that. Because it's a smaller city, it feels like you can do more. The work is more visible. That continues to give me energy to keep doing it."

Katie admits she is "susceptible to utopian visions," and that susceptibility has extended into a decade-long study of the Shaker communities that grew around New England in the 1800s. An egalitarian, collective-based spiritual group started by Mother

Annabel Lee, "the only woman to pioneer an American religious communal experiment that lasted longer than one generation,"[5] the Shakers embraced many of the values Katie tries to uphold in her own life. "I've gone to a couple of the old Shaker villages," she says. "Obviously they were really extreme, because they felt the kingdom was upon us. But the way they lived collectively and the egalitarianism and gender balance and pacifism and integrated schools are amazing to me." Shaker schools did not teach religion, and their spirituality included the idea that Annabel Lee "was possessed of the same spirit as Jesus," as Katie puts it. But the Shakers were also a celibate community, which caused their membership to wither as people died off or left the community to pursue marriage and children. However, their decision-making process appeals to Katie. In the Shaker communities "everything was egalitarian. Only highly specialized things would sit with one person. There were two male elders and two female elders. They were a way station for runaway slaves. To me, I feel like except for the second coming and lack of procreation, I don't see much wrong with it."

"And that for me," she continues, "is a good example of how I don't bear ill will toward religion. I think the community aspect of religion can be so strong. But that's what makes it terrifying and dangerous." Katie's antiauthoritarian and community-based stances color her response to religion's hierarchical structure, but as she says, "I wish the Shakers were still around" to provide a counterpoint of how religion could work in a better way. "I don't think religion is the driver of those structures," she says, "but it is a good buttress, so to speak."

When I ask if there are any final thoughts she'd like to add, Katie pauses. "There's one thing that's important," she finally says. "I definitely don't hate religion. I can identify as an atheist, but I don't have strong anti-religious feelings. The only place where it gets extremely contentious are things like Creationism in the class-

---

[5] D'Ann Campbell, "Women's Life in Utopia: The Shaker Experiment in Sexual Equality Reappraised, 1810–1860," *New England Quarterly* 5/1 (March 1978).

room and the Religious Right's power over legislation. Whatever people need to get by, as long as it doesn't hurt other people, it's fine. That's why I don't identify loudly as an atheist, because it comes off as a judgment on people who aren't, and I'm not trying to take that stance." She admits that it's difficult for her when religious people "push their judgment" on nonbelievers, because she works hard not to do the same. However, she adds, "everybody has whatever beliefs they're going to have, and it's really hard to live in the world. Anything people can do that makes them feel like they're being fed is fantastic."

2

Belonging without Believing

The old cliche that "there are no atheists in foxholes" might best be reframed today; there are indeed atheists in foxholes, because the US Army added "humanist" as a religious preference for soldiers in April 2014. However, in July of the same year, the US Navy rejected an application from a candidate for the position of chaplain who self-identified as a humanist, raising an outcry from secular groups and nonbelieving service members.[1] Self-identification as a none, atheist, or agnostic has gone from a private decision to an issue of public debate. After facing public mockery and rejection in more close-minded times, those who do not belong to an institutional religion are asking to be granted the same rights as their believing counterparts.

But if there are atheists in foxholes, are they also in church? It's impossible to calculate how many nonbelievers, doubters, or seekers might be sitting in a synagogue, mosque, or church, but based on averages, chances are that there are more than a few. There is also a growing interest among some nonbelievers to form an alternate sort of church, a place they can gather and move through some of the same rituals of belief they may have left behind, build community ties, and engage in social activism.

The first time I read about Sunday Assembly, what caught my attention was the fact that it was founded by two British stand-up comedians. I imagined some sort of Andy Kaufman–esque

---

[1] Michelle Boorstein, "Secular Group Protests Navy's Rejection of Humanist Chaplain," *Washington Post*, June 18, 2014.

meta-joke: "Let's start an atheist church and see if anyone figures out what that means!" As I was lugging my own growing agnosticism along when I bothered to show up for church, the idea that people would voluntarily enact something akin to the very set of rituals and creeds that was alienating me and most of the people I was interviewing was puzzling. Why would anyone, especially people who'd deliberately exited organized religion, attend an atheist church?

The answer is complicated. Even after departing organized religion, many nonbelievers miss what was good about it. Among the people I spoke to, those things tended to fall into the same categories: community was foremost, followed by ritual or some sort of repeated set of actions, and often a sense of social engagement. Churches excel at providing aid in disasters. And churches can also be good at creating the kind of social ties that many people experience as severely lacking in our increasingly isolated culture, an isolation arguably exacerbated by technology. So why not put technology to work creating a different model of what it means to be a church?

From the beginning the creators of the Sunday Assembly used social media with the savvy inherent to digital natives. Click open the average church website and you're greeted by clunky design, digital clip-art graphics, grainy video of an ill-attended service, a low-quality audio file of a sermon, and almost no interactive features. In contrast, the Sunday Assembly site looks as if it was designed by a twenty-five-year-old. Its slick design is matched by its seamless interactivity, with a clickable map of worldwide Sunday Assembly gatherings, links to Facebook, a live Twitter feed, and most impressively, really snappy slogans. "A global network of people who want to make the most of this one life we know we have." "Our mission: to help everyone find and fulfill their full potential." And the one that most reflects Sunday Assembly's roots in stand-up comedy, "It's all the best bits of religion, but with no religion, and awesome pop songs!" Sure, Sunday Assembly has just under five thousand Twitter followers to Pope Francis's almost six million, but the organizers also show every sign of understanding how to appeal to a younger demographic.

In the case of Sunday Assembly, the tactic has worked—to a point. Many Millennials and Gen-Xers have in common a hefty dose of skepticism and cynicism about whether things like an afterlife or reincarnation, the backbone of many organized religions, have anything to do with the way their lives should be lived now. Sanderson Jones, one of the cofounders of Sunday Assembly, told the BBC that thinking of life as a one-time deal gives him a sense of consolation. "We come from nothing and we go to nothing. . . . If you don't believe in God, that just makes life more precious."[2] Jones admits that, apart from the secular songs that are sung and the absence of prayers, Sunday Assembly does in many ways act like a church: "We just nicked the order of service," he told the BBC.

From the beginning Jones and Pippa Evans, the cofounder, infused the movement with a DIY spirit. On the Sunday Assembly website you can download a "Public Charter" that explains the thinking behind the gatherings. The website promises that a "Road Map for New Assemblies," to guide people through starting their own iterations, and an "Accreditation Model," which, they admit, they've had "some difficulties finding the best way to go ahead with," are forthcoming. Another difficulty, as with organized religion in general, has been getting enough money. A crowd-funded drive to raise £500,000 (nearly a million US dollars) instead raised only £33,000. Yet more cities have begun offering a Sunday Assembly. So, rather like most movements in their infancy, this one is growing slowly, struggling to pay its way.

The idea of an atheist church is not entirely new. Unitarian Universalists have long held services that welcome atheists and agnostics. Unitarians even have a web page explicitly inviting nonbelievers into participation; on it, Rev. Dr. William Schulz, president of the UU Service Committee, writes, "[Unitarians] believe that human beings are responsible for the future; that history is in our hands, not those of an angry God or inexorable fate."[3]

---

[2] Quoted in Robert Pigott, "Doing Church without God," *BBC News,* November 1, 2013.

[3] "Atheist and Agnostic People Welcome," Unitarian Universalist Association (UUA), http://www.uua.org.

Positivist philosopher August Comte tried to found a godless religion in the early 1800s, writing a treatise calling for the founding of a "Religion of Humanity." Comte explicitly considered his Religion of Humanity to be "catholicism without Christ" and instead to be "catholicism plus science," but the otherwise esoteric ideas behind Comte's religion meant that it never grew beyond a few adherents, and one source even says that Comte "accomplished a tour de force by uniting both believers and nonbelievers against him."[4] There are many other examples of humanist, atheist, and agnostic congregations, but aside from Unitarians, the majority describe themselves as believers (although Unitarians I spoke to usually described God as a symbol rather than an entity), no godless alternative to organized religion has ever lasted for long and developed a truly sustainable congregation.

The East Bay Sunday Assembly started having meetings in January 2014, and its website shows that they meet monthly. In addition to music (Sunday Assembly's theme song is Queen's "Don't Stop Me Now"), every gathering features a guest speaker; July's was the managing director of a robotics startup, and August's was a psychologist speaking about how wonder relates to education. *Wonder* is a key word the Assembly founders use with the same frequency that Christians use the word *faith. Wonder* implies a kind of joyful engagement with the mysteries of life and lends to the tone of many Assembly talks and interviews a kind of childlike awe that may be part of why it appeals to young Millennials in particular. But when I asked Sam, the atheist from the previous chapter, if he would ever attend something like that regularly, his answer was a firm no. The point of a pseudoreligious gathering was beyond his range of interest. I also queried another friend about whether she would be likely to participate. Like Sam, she'd been raised without organized religion in a rural, hippie family, but she'd married a Unitarian who missed some of the "leftie church" feeling of the UU. She has a four-year-old son and is looking for ways to build community as a parent. But she, too, was

---

[4] Michel Bourdeau, "Auguste Comte," *Stanford Encyclopedia of Philosophy,* http://plato.stanford.edu.

skeptical, although she admitted that it might be a weird feeling if she attended something like a Sunday Assembly and liked it. For someone with little interest in mainstream religion, what would that mean? The fact that she was so skeptical about the questions that attending a godless gathering might raise was enough to keep her, and likely others, far away from a Sunday Assembly meeting.

If Sunday Assembly is one model for an alternative to church, its being in its infancy means that while it fills the hole of providing a community, it will be hard to convince some nonbelievers that a church-like service is the way to do that. But what about our atheists and doubters in foxholes? Not all of them want to join an atheist church; some still show up at churches, synagogues, and mosques, and some even attend seminary and divinity school, in spite of their doubts about God. Can a person participate in religion without being a believer? And, if so, what do such people gain, and what do they lose?

Matthew calls me from what sounds like a busy street corner in an East Coast city. Traffic, conversations, and the noise of a densely populated urban area pipe in through the receiver underneath his voice. He speaks in a torrent, words spilling out quickly and urgently, as if there is much to say and a limited time to say it in. A mutual friend had suggested he get in touch with me, and after a couple of scheduling emails, we set a date to talk. I knew that Matthew worked with a Jewish organization and had attended divinity school, but I also knew that he was open about his atheism, and I was curious as to how he balanced those two things.

"Four years ago I started to identify as an atheist," he says. Matthew went to divinity school and graduated in 2009. However, "for a long time I'd struggled with belief and how to figure out my concept of God. About a year after I graduated, I was at a dinner party and the topic of God came up. Someone who didn't know me well just asked me if I believed in God. For years I'd been giving complicated answers, and I'd gotten tired of that. So I just said no." Matthew explains that in spite of a lifetime of doubt, before that moment he had never consciously thought of himself as a nonbeliever. "I don't pray, and my concept of God is so far gone I can't explain it in a useful manner," he says. Admitting that he had lost God "was a little shocking and led to a professional crisis." Matthew had been working in Jewish education and was "headed down that path." But the revelation of his atheism felt at that moment like an insurmountable obstacle.

Matthew was raised "sort of conservative Jewish. I took it seriously, and at about twelve I decided to be Orthodox. I became very religious, keeping Shabbat, keeping Kashrut," which means following the Jewish dietary laws. "But," he adds, "I didn't have a community." After about four years of religious fervor and explorations of Jewish Orthodoxy, around the age of sixteen, he "just stopped praying as much." However, he attended a Jewish theological seminary for college, and that's when his faith really began to unravel in earnest. "When I learned biblical criticism, that was the beginning of the end," he says. "My basis for belief was about the revelation on Sinai and once that was no longer trustworthy"—once he realized that it could be picked apart—"I couldn't say what God was like."

Matthew's divinity studies continued to cause difficulty in his ability to define God. "Three things had a major impact" in his growing definition of himself as an atheist. "Catholic mysticism and negative theology," also known as apophatic theology, or the attempt to understand God by discerning what God is not, "which to me is atheistic," Matthew says. "I studied with Gordon Kauffman, who was into constructive theology. That played a big role in finding myself out" as a nonbeliever. He also took a class called "Theology and the Death of God," and read Richard Kearney's *Anatheism,* which posits that we are living in a time of "God after God," and that the "free decision to believe or not believe is not just tolerated but cherished."[5] Matthew's time in divinity school and introduction to radical ways of thinking about God also caused him to consider whether God was more of a description than a

---

[5] Richard Kearney, "Preface," in *Anatheism: Returning to God after God* (New York: Columbia University Press, 2011), xiv.

person, place, or thing. "Sometimes you use the word *God*," he says, "but sometimes the word *divinity* or the word *sacred*. So it was interesting seeing it treated as an adjective and not a noun." With that comprehension, "the word *God* was no longer helpful" to Matthew.

When I ask how it felt to "come out" to his family as an atheist, Matthew laughs and says "coming out" is the exact term he uses. When he revealed his newfound atheism, "usually people said 'you didn't [already] know you were an atheist'?" Throughout his process of discerning his nonbelief, he had been "struggling and talking" with his family. His father greeted the news by saying that he was already an atheist himself. His mother was "concerned in some sense," because she wanted him to retain a commitment to his "Jewish identity and community."

And keeping in touch with his roots and culture is exactly what Matthew did, even after he left God behind. "I'm part of a community in Boston," he says, "Moishe/Kavod House. It's a very special community, sort of an informal synagogue with a social justice agenda." Moishe/Kavod House is part of an international network of sixty-one houses and describes itself as having a special emphasis on *Tikkun olam,* a Hebrew phrase that emphasizes humanity's shared responsibility in healing the world. Of his participation at Moishe/Kavod, Matthew says, "I do everything but go to services. I taught a session on the retreat, I make food, socialize, do political things, but I don't pray with them."

Matthew also keeps engaged in Judaism through his work as a teacher and writer, although his pedagogical emphasis on secularism has meant that "I had to leave Judaism as a professional career." "On an institutional level," he says, "I only teach at places that allow me to teach what I want. I teach high school students, a class called 'Ecclesiastes and Existentialism.' I teach a series of theology courses, [including] theology for skeptics. I teach people to use the tradition to work through the journey of faith." When I ask if his atheism ever affects his relationships with religious Jews or other believers he encounters, Matthew says, "I mostly keep in situations where I'm the most studied person on the topic, so there is not much struggle. I have friends who are rabbis and divinity students, but there's no hardship. It's very loving and supportive. If anything," he says, "people approach me as a resource."

Before we spoke, Matthew had directed me to his blog. One phrase that he had used in several blog entries caught my eye: "God shaped longing." I ask him to elaborate on this, and he's eloquent in his response. This is obviously something he's considered at length. "There's a place in our heads that works into our hearts, a desire for ultimacy," he says. Humans desire "security and cosmic orientation. Just because I'm a nonbeliever doesn't mean I don't love those things. I had a God for a long time, but I'm committed to not having something take God's place. Humanists sometimes forget that if we take God out, we're at the top. That God-shaped hole for me is a recognition that without God there are a lot of spaces, questions that don't have answers, and I want to safeguard that and not fill it in with something like work or country. I've grown to be comfortable with that. I'm uncomfortable with people who try to fill that."

Since coming out as an atheist, Matthew has found a way to be comfortable in the liminal space of participating in Jewish rituals while still advocating for, writing about, and teaching others about secularism and spirituality. But he admits that this can be difficult for others to parse. "What's tricky is that if you see religion as an affiliation and set of behaviors, I'm actually religious," he says. "I'm secular and religious and atheist. I just celebrated Shavuot," the day God gave the Torah to the people of Israel. "I'm religiously practicing," he says, but "I just don't pray. I just don't bring God into it at any point." When I ask if this is for him a kind of DIY religion, he says no. "I'm not making up a new spirituality," he says, winding up our conversation as he heads off to teach a class. "I'm just being Jewish."

Like Matthew, Meredith's questioning and doubt about God began at an inconvenient time. When she enrolled in divinity school, Meredith was confronted with the radically different culture of New England and the surrounding religious differences from her evangelical Southern Baptist upbringing; it resulted in a cascade of unanswerable questions she is still struggling with today.

Meredith is a musician and writer, studying in a nondenominational track rather than an ordination track. We spoke in the morning, before she headed off to a day of classes. Her fellowship is from her school's sacred music institute, and from the beginning, she's been interested in the intersection of theology and art. But that combination, which comes so naturally to many believers, has resulted in some static with the church she grew up in. "I had a great experience," she says. "My church supports me financially, emotionally, and spiritually." But upon further reflection, Meredith says that her drift from her Southern Baptist roots began before she arrived at divinity school. "Yeah," she says with a kind of half sigh, "I sort of moved away. Felt myself moving away in college." While doing a college internship at a church in Nashville focusing on creative liturgy, she found that "integrating art into liturgy caused me to move away from Southern Baptists. Art wasn't shunned, but it wasn't important. Augustine thought that beauty and art lead to temptation, not to God. But I kept seeing art as my main source to God."

In her undergrad years Meredith majored in religion and art at Belmont University, a liberal arts Christian college in Nashville with a long list of notable musical alumni. But, like Matthew, college was the "first time I was exposed to criticism of biblical texts, and I started questioning what I grew up believing." She began graduate studies "straight out of undergrad," and describes it as a time of "moving away from the evangelical church in a social context. My beliefs about God," she says, "were different from my peers," who were mainly Episcopalians and Mainline Protestants.

"I guess you could say I'm searching," she says. "I'm open to denominations, but I'm still figuring out what I believe about that. Young people are moving away from labels and deciding how we group ourselves religiously." Divinity school has meant for Meredith a further consideration of what it means to belong to a religious tradition that doesn't necessarily square with her internal identification. When I ask if she's seriously considering a change in religion now that she's away from other Southern Baptists, she replies, "I'm deciding if it's important that I hook myself up to anything. Do I want to commit and walk with people regardless of leadership?" Like many Millennials, Meredith feels she fits in with many religions, rather than one, and as a result, she finds it difficult to commit to any of them. "Some groups I'm more at home with. Presbyterians and Episcopalians, ironically," because those are the predominant ones in her area. "In the South," she says, "your denomination's either Christian or Catholic."

The liminal space of what Meredith now calls her "none-ness" has created some distance between her and her classmates. "I'm not the norm here," she admits. "Not to say there aren't other students that are confused and discerning, but the majority that came from a denomination like I did have swung in another direction. Most have picked something and committed." She notes that many of her classmates are LGBTQ, which is an "important factor" in their finding a denomination in which they can be out and be in ministry. Coming from a denomination that does not ordain women, Meredith says she feels "that same pressure to align with a faith that aligns with my belief on those issues." Her faculty members have not made this any easier, because they continue to check in with her as to where she is in her search. Meredith says that this feels like a "pressure to find something in order that I can be ghettoized into my appropriate divinity-school camp, because at this point I don't fit anywhere."

Backtracking to her earlier point about young people moving away from labels about their faith lives, Meredith says, "That's a hard conversation to have up here. People are sensitive to it. It's not easy to articulate in my own community. Some people feel that kind of thinking might be a personal attack on their vocational choice." The outside pressure she feels right now is more about finding a group she can fit into, "and the ordaining question."

Coming from Catholicism myself, where women's ordination is a painful issue for several close friends, I ask her to define what ordination means to her. "At this point I don't necessarily feel a call," she says, "but realize even as a woman if I went back to my own denomination, that call comes from God and not from a church. Being ordained is something I could be blessed with before a church or committee can do it." For now, Meredith is at peace with the idea that she may not end up as a priest or a reverend. "Coming to terms with that has been helpful for me in reconciling this place of none-ness. There's a place for me in ministry that's been ordained by God." However, surrounded by so many divinity students who are pursuing ordination, "it does make it difficult to fit in. But that's more social. I don't go to church, really, so that's weird to say out loud. It's the first time in my life when Sunday mornings aren't an assumed time to go. Finding my church in other ways has been helpful. For me, church is having a good conversation over coffee with a friend, or taking a walk and paying attention; not to sound hippy dippy, but I have to find church in other ways."

Meredith had described herself as a None several times during our conversation, so I asked her to talk about going into ministry while being religiously ambiguous. "I felt totally out of place," she says of arriving at divinity school. "This young girl who grew up in a conservative place, with old ladies from home sending me Facebook messages that the devil would take over my soul. But at the same time, such a strong sense of this being where I was supposed to be. It's reconciling where I am," she says, "all a part of a bigger journey, and this season is part of that growing process." She mentions that she's been reading Simone Weil, the French philosopher, activist, and Christian mystic, who Meredith describes as "so dramatic." But Weil's description of atheism as a "trial that all Christians go through" resonates deeply with Meredith's doubt. Later, I dig up the quotation from Weil:

Religion in so far as it is a source of consolation is a hindrance to true faith; and in this sense atheism is a purification. I have to be an atheist with that part of myself which is not made for God. Among those in whom the supernatural part of themselves has not been awakened, the atheists are right and the believers wrong.[6]

---

[6] Simone Weil, "Faiths of Meditation: A Contemplation of the Divine," in *The Simone Weil Reader*, ed. George A. Panichas (New York: David McKay, 1977), 417.

"I feel like I'm going through that," Meredith says. "There are more days when I question if I have a sense of God, and I'm in divinity school. I talk twelve hours a day about God and come home and ask if it's [nonsense]. But" she adds, "I think walking this through and reconciling this season of doubt and pilgrimage is just about trusting this is what it's supposed to be. Coming here was the right next step. The steps after that," she admits, "I'm not equipped to consider."

Since I know that she's studying the relationship between music and faith, and that she's also taking a writing course, I ask Meredith to say more about the role of creativity in her "season of doubt."

"Art has really been the only way I've been able to understand God," she says. She describes the concept of God being so abstract that art was the only thing that allowed her to wrap her mind around it. "It's been a way to use something physical and palpable and rich to help me interpret something so far away." Meredith began her understanding of art and divinity during her childhood, when she was "a weirdly religious kid baptizing my sisters in the bathtub. As a kid I found allegorical things about God in the *Jungle Book* and theater." Later, music became her primary avenue of expression, but now, "writing and literature seem more helpful." Meredith had recently published an essay, and she described the impetus for writing it as knit up with her confusing experiences in divinity school.

"The article is about denomination," she says. "What do you do when your portrait of God is altered or changed?" She asks if I've heard of *asperging,* and I admit the word is unfamiliar. She describes it as "using something like a palm branch or broom to wave holy water around," and an image of a priest swinging branches around arises in my mind, which I let her know. Of her first months at divinity school she says, "I used to have conversations about my evangelical background that really scared people, and those things that seemed normal to me seemed outrageous or cultish to my peers. So I go to community chapel, and they did the holy water thing, and they didn't explain it, but all of a sudden this woman priest picks up this witches' broom thing and I got drenched in this water. I was so thrown off," Meredith says, "I walked out and cried in the bathroom. It was very off-putting, but it started this journey of reconciling my understanding of God with other people's traditions. Do I allow this to open up a new understanding? Through writing that story," she says, "I was able to make those things true for me."

Matthew and Meredith are religiously "in between." Both continue to participate in religion, and both see themselves as people with vocational callings. But their respective atheism and doubt put them in tenuous positions within organized religion. Matthew is able to participate in community with other young Jewish people and even to teach classes about Judaism, but he cannot honestly commit himself to attending synagogue as an atheist. Meredith is still on the path to completing her master of divinity degree and working within the framework of organized religion, but the pressure to choose a denomination and her drifting from the denomination of her upbringing have sent her into a tailspin of doubt about God. Both of them hit the hard, life-changing moment of doubt in divinity school, logically a time when a person's commitment to faith would thicken and deepen. But in both these cases, it shattered.

Many people I spoke to said that when they hit a difficult moment, as Matthew or Meredith did, the religions they belonged to failed to allow them to spend time dealing with doubts and questions. Institutions like churches, synagogues, and mosques often showed little patience for searchers and doubters, and as a result, those searchers and doubters gave up on the search. Further complications arose when the search began in childhood. As interfaith marriages increase, more and more children are raised to be "both/and." But is it possible to really practice two religions at once, or does the pressure to discern which one is "correct" push younger people even further away? Or, in some cases, can they find a way to blend enough bits and pieces from multiple faiths to create something sustaining? The more people I spoke to, the more a common theme arose out of our conversations: tension. These people experienced the tension of family, the tension of social judgment about belonging or not belonging, and the self-imposed tension about making a choice whether God was real or not. And tension, as we all know, is not a comfortable experience to inhabit for long. Increasingly, however, with the loss of cultural and social ties to a single faith, many people's experience of religion as a state of tension shows signs of becoming permanent.

3

Liminal Faith

On a warm February day in 2014, the winter sun flaring a reminder of earth's increasingly rapid tilt toward self-incineration, I got into the car with my husband and drove us to my niece's bat mitzvah. It wasn't until the early 2000s that it became clear that my family, for generations stalwartly Irish Catholic, was following the lead of many other American families and becoming something religiously in-between. I was back in the Catholic Church, albeit uneasily, but my four siblings and mother had long ago headed for the exit doors. My mother, who had worked in the Native American community for decades, absented herself from Catholicism after my father's death in favor of a humanist/natural world mishmash. My oldest sister married a convert to Zen Buddhism and didn't bother with religion herself. My brother was a once-in-a-while churchgoer married to a non-churchgoer. My other older sister preferred nature and camping to religion and married an atheist. I married an agnostic. And then my younger sister married a Jewish guy.

Although my brother-in-law went to medical school in Israel, his family is probably best described as very loosely Jewish. His own bar mitzvah had been casual and informal; it took place in his living room. I'd been to his father's house for a Seder, and while we followed the ritual, it was also a shambolic affair, with kids coming and going, songs half sung, and piety largely ditched in favor of enjoyment. But over the years an unexpected thing happened: my eldest niece became deeply religious. She excelled at Hebrew, wanted to observe all the Jewish holidays, and asked to be sent to a Chabad

(Orthodox) summer camp. When she befriended an Orthodox girl in her class, my niece began wearing long sleeves and long pants even on hot days. When it came time for a bat mitzvah, she took it seriously, cracking down even harder on her Hebrew and cutting off her waist-length hair to donate it to a group that makes wigs for cancer patients as a *mitzvah* (good deed). My sister's family joined a Conservative synagogue, a middle ground between Reform and Orthodox, and that's where my niece's bat mitzvah took place.

Watching my niece carry the Torah scroll around the synagogue, wrapped in a prayer shawl sewn by my ex-Catholic mother, I noticed that most of my family members had given up trying to follow along in the Siddur in favor of half-chanting along in a mangled Hebrew/English hybrid. When one of my niece's uncles from her father's side of the family got up to read from the Torah, he struggled through the Hebrew and actually said "this is hard" aloud at one point, soliciting giggles from the congregation. A Shabbat service, into which the bat mitzvah is folded, is not that different from a Catholic mass, minus the Eucharist, of course; there are prayers, songs, and a talk by the rabbi. The bat mitzvah, however, is much more rigorous than my own Catholic confirmation had been: my niece did several Hebrew readings, and wrote and delivered a Midrash on a tricky passage from Exodus. But there were common threads between her religion and mine, and she'd heard me deliver a reflection at a Catholic mass, so I gave her Midrash a thumbs up from my seat. Maybe seeing my atheist brother-in-law in a yarmulke, sitting in a house of worship, was a little weird; seeing my agnostic husband in a yarmulke was also weird, even though he did the best job out of all of us of following the songs in the Siddur. But seeing them within the context of a family celebrating my niece's reception into the religion she embraced so wholeheartedly? In that framework it made perfect sense. Even the rabbi mentioned that my niece was among many kids in the schul with a non-Jewish mother who still participated in the life of the community. Maybe we aren't Jewish, but we are all part of the web of relationships that will help define how my niece sees and understands faith. My niece will most likely choose to remain Jewish, but perhaps, coming out of an interfaith marriage and being part of a religiously eclectic family, her faith will be shaded and colored by the people she's surrounded by.

Whether that kind of religious mixology is good or bad for the children of interfaith families remains a subject of debate, but this much is true: they are a growing segment of the population. A report from the Council on Contemporary Families (CCF) states that "the proportion of individuals who marry a partner from a different religious tradition (including ones with no religious upbringing) has risen steadily, from just over 40 percent in the 1960s to as much as 55 percent by the early 2000s."[1] The researchers argue this may be a reflection of a "loosening of social boundaries" in America, but in an increasing percentage of these interfaith relationships, rather than converting, the partners have chosen to maintain separate religious practices. Mormons are the least likely to marry a partner from a different religion or to maintain separate religious practices if they do, whereas same-sex married partners are the most likely to accept a spouse from a different religious background; for example, 74 percent of same-sex male couples maintain religious differences. Unsurprisingly, given Millennials' greater openness to interracial and same-sex relationships, religious miscegenation is greeted with approval by Millennials. According to the CCF report, 80 percent of them approve of interfaith marriage. With that level of approval it's increasingly likely that the future children of Millennials, and the current children of Gen Xers, will grow up religiously "both/and."

Susan Katz-Miller, herself the product of an interfaith family (Episcopalian mother, Jewish father), claimed Judaism as her chosen religion, married an Episcopalian, and has chosen to raise her kids in both religions. In *On Being Both,* Katz-Miller interviews many interfaith families and comes down firmly on the side that raising children in more than one religion is good for the child and for the extended family. "In an interfaith setting," she writes, "both parents have equal status; neither parent feels like the out-parent.

---

[1] David McClendon, "CCF Civil Rights Symposium: Interfaith Marriage and Romantic Unions in the United States," Council on Contemporary Families, February 4, 2014, https://contemporaryfamilies.org.

Both parents can sit at a gathering or holiday celebration with the children, and neither will feel like a guest."[2] Near the end of the book Katz-Miller interviews a range of Millennials raised in interfaith homes and paints a fairly rosy picture of their ability to feel at home in more than one religion. The majority, she writes, desire to stay "both," and very few of them feel the pressure to choose one of their faiths over another. Many of them are "defending their right to formulate religious identities at their own pace and on their own terms."[3]

That final statement resonates with the stories of many interfaith people I spoke with. Raised in two religions or two denominations, they are taking time to discern what role faith will play in their lives, and along the way they are asking questions about what it really means to believe. But by choosing to take their time in this process, they are also defying the expectations of older generations of American society, some of whom feel that they lack commitment. At a panel on the state of American faith at the Aspen Institute in June 2014, *The New Republic*'s former editor Leon Wieseltier told an audience member who asked a question about her own interfaith family that "what worries me is that the new forms will be so disconnected from the traditions; that something called Judaism will survive, but that the tradition in its richness may not. That is my deepest fear about my faith." At the same panel historian Molly Worthern critiqued the "problem with the hyper-individualization of Millennial religion. The advantage of an institution is that it . . . forces you to grapple with a tradition that includes hard ideas. It forces you to have, for at least part of your life, a respect for authority that inculcates the sense that you have something to learn, that you're not reinventing the wheel, but that millennia have come before you. The structure of institutions, for all their evils, facilitates that. And we may be losing that."[4] But

---

[2] Susan Katz Miller, *Being Both: Embracing Two Religions in One Interfaith Family* (Boston: Beacon Press, 2013), 42.

[3] Ibid., 203.

[4] Quoted in Conor Friedersdorf, "The Case Against Mix-and-Match Spirituality," *The Atlantic,* June 28, 2014.

the children of interfaith relationships don't just grapple with one institution; they grapple with two or more. They engage more hard ideas and deal with more questions of authority. Does that mean they have more choices to make as adults about which of those authorities they will place their trust in? Yes, it does. And that is why many of them take their time choosing which path they will ultimately follow, or if they will follow more than one, or create their own. In that time many of them transition into a liminal faith.

Carolyn is twenty-six. She lives on the East Coast and works for a religiously affiliated nonprofit organization. Raised in a household with an Evangelical Lutheran mother and a "very secular" Jewish father, Carolyn absorbed bits and pieces of two religions throughout her childhood. When I asked if there had ever been any discussion about choosing one religion or another, Carolyn replied that her "mom said she would have been okay with the kids being Jewish, but dad said no." Instead, Carolyn went to her mother's church but frankly says, "I didn't like the church we went to very much. . . . It wasn't bad but it wasn't awesome." Her mother still attends a church in the same denomination, but after her confirmation at fourteen, Carolyn "just kind of peaced out."

What led to that "peacing out"? "I think not going was mostly my own doubts and not really enjoying the church," Carolyn replies. "I liked confirmation classes, but I didn't like waking up early. And when you're obligated to go . . . you're less likely to absorb stuff." Her skepticism about churchgoing started when she was very young. "I had doubts starting in maybe fourth grade," she admits. Carolyn's childhood church was mostly an aging congregation, so her Sunday School classes were small. And there was an awareness, even from a young age, that "Lutherans felt wishy washy to me. At least Catholics had the guts to stay stuff even if I didn't agree, but Lutherans . . . " She pauses for a minute before continuing. "There was volunteering and stuff, but nothing that really pumped me up." Like many kids forced to attend churches that didn't do much to make their time there worthwhile, Carolyn's interest faded fast. Her mother told her that once she made it through confirmation, it was okay "to go off now." So she did.

In high school Carolyn began volunteering at Planned Parenthood, "one of the few clinics that did abortions" in the area of the Midwest where she grew up. On many days when she showed up to volunteer "there would be protesters, and they didn't help my feelings toward organized religion in general." Volunteering at Planned Parenthood did, however, lead to a continued engagement in issues of women's rights. But her dismay about religions picketing and trying to block access to the clinic didn't prepare her for the strange turn her faith life took when she went off to college.

"So, college," she says. "If you told me I was going to get involved with this cool church I would have laughed." By then, she'd moved so far from organized religion that it didn't appeal to her in the least. But she was attending a Christian-affiliated university, and during midterms, when she was "bummed out, on a Thursday night at 11 I went into the chapel, and there was a healing service happening hosted by the Methodist campus ministry." A young woman invited her in, and the darkened chapel was filled with candlelight. "It was soothing," she recalls. "I'd heard the pastor speak in a class before, so I introduced myself, and that was about halfway through freshman year." Carolyn wound up working in a "de facto Mainline Protestant organization" on campus after that night. "There was an even more evangelical group that would meet," she says, "but I didn't hang out with them." The Methodist umbrella group that ran campus ministry "pulled in a lot of different groups" and offered her a different kind of engagement in religion than she'd had as a child at an aging parish. This time, she discovered a peer-based one. "I had a couple of different roles. Hospitality coordinator, treasurer, my senior year I was co-worship coordinator. And that was cool. It was a fun group of people to do that kind of thing with."

Her experience working in campus ministry motivated her to learn more about the other side of her interfaith background. She signed up to spend a semester abroad in Israel during her junior year. "I was thinking I'd get in touch with my Jewish half and have a profound spiritual experience," she says, "and none of those things happened." Like many interfaith kids, Carolyn's experience had been one of greater exposure to one parent's religion, but Israeli culture rebuffed her efforts to discover what it might mean to be both Jewish and Christian. "Everything was high pressure and very black and white religiously and politically," she says. There were a lot of discussions about intermarriage, not specifically about me or my parents. I'm sympathetic to leaders' concerns about that. I can understand it as a minority faith. But I heard so much about it that kind of distanced me." The division of sexes often seen in Orthodox Judaism was also difficult for her to negotiate, like seeing men and women praying in different sections at the Wailing Wall, or discussions of how some commandments applied to men and others to women. The fact that Carolyn's father is Jewish, and therefore she is not technically Jewish herself, because Jewish heritage is traced matrilineally, "got really awkward," she recalls. "It pushed me away from faith." Years later, she realizes that she wasn't prepared for the challenges Israel would pose for her interfaith experience. "I didn't have the perspective I have now that you determine your own religious identity."

After Carolyn's graduation from college she briefly lived with a roommate from her campus ministry years and attended a Methodist church, but after she moved a further distance from that "older and wealthier" parish, "nothing was particularly compelling that helped me continue to come back." Thus began a long and ongoing stretch of trying to find a church where Carolyn fit in and felt at home. One parish seemed promising for someone who doesn't like "to get up early," but the slick video screen and pop music soundtrack of a "youth church" didn't work for her either. "They didn't have hymnals, and I didn't like singing lyrics off of a screen." Another try at a different friend's parish landed her there during a sermon series week with a focus on "social justice heroes" with no mention of the gospel whatsoever. A different parish offered a Christian Seder service, but a Seder framed in a Christian context didn't make sense to Carolyn. She tried going back to a Lutheran church similar to the one she'd attended as a child but "heard some anti-Semitic stuff" on Good Friday and never returned.

"I do and I don't have an ideal church," she says. "I also used to attend Shabbat services and that's always struck me as interesting and compelling." Carolyn admits she "only has a bit of Hebrew" but prefers a traditional style of Shabbat or parish service. "The assumption about young adults and music," she says, "is aaaaaaargh. I like traditional hymns. I like a traditional service. But," she adds, "I'd like a more liberal theology." Carolyn's search for a faith she can stick with "comes and goes." "Right now it's on the back burner," she says, but she also admits that whenever she stops attending services, she "feels a little flaky. But there's a burnout issue there too," she admits. At one point she'd found a good balance—"I was focused on a prayer journal and did a regular mix of Shabbat and church services and met with a rabbi about converting at an all-purpose synagogue." She currently works for a lay-run Christian organization, and while she's pretty sure that she's not interested in becoming a member of this particular denomination herself, encountering people who stay in the church while disagreeing with church leadership on some issues has been an eye-opener for her. "It's given me a lot more understanding that it's okay to be part of a community you have profound disagreements with," she says. "It's been useful in that regard. We talk a lot about conscience, and that's something I don't think you see a ton in other religious traditions. Maybe I haven't encountered it. But this idea that conscience is extremely important. This whole thing about you don't have to fit into a box," she says, "has been useful and a relief."

Carolyn is currently dating a man who identifies as an atheist, "but not an asshole," she adds with a laugh. After one of their first dates, she was poking around his Facebook page and saw mention of a book by "Christopher Hitchens or one of the angry atheists," and thought to herself, "this is going to be an adventure." But being paired with an atheist hasn't posed any problems so far. "He's been super mellow" about her explorations of faith. "I don't think he'd be surprised or object to my exploring different communities," she says. And just as her mother allowed her father to stay home for all those Sundays of churchgoing, Carolyn says of her boyfriend, "I wouldn't expect him to come along" if she did find a regular religious practice. However, for now, she remains religiously in between. She experiments with different forms of prayer, writes about her faith life, and tries out a different parish or tradition once in a while. Statistically, this puts Carolyn in the minority of Nones; only 10 percent of the Nones surveyed by PEW describe themselves as "looking for a religion that would be right for you."[5] The vast majority say they are not looking for a religion. Is this a position of discomfort for her, or a liminal space that threatens to become permanent? Not really. It's just how things have turned out, and for now, it works.

Not every interfaith person comes from a family that splits between two different faiths. Many are from what older generations referred to as mixed marriages: Catholic and Protestant or two different Protestant sects. With their radically different ways of approaching faith, however, the difference between a more evangelical Protestantism and Mainline Protestantism can feel, for the children of those families, like emerging from two completely different religions. And for some of those kids, growing into adulthood means emerging out of religion altogether. This reflects a larger demographic bleed out of Protestantism. In the early 1970s, more than 60 percent of Americans described themselves as active participants in a Protestant church. By 2012, 51 percent said the same thing.[6] For some children born into families that mix different forms of Protestantism, the vast feeling of difference between, for example, the liberal Mainline United Church of Christ and the fiery rhetoric of Pentecostalism can create so much static about what religion should mean that it is easier to walk away than to choose one or the other.

Cassandra and I speak across the distance of a handful of states. She lives in the Midwest; after having moved around through her

---

[5] "'Nones' on the Rise," Pew Research Center, October 9, 2012, http://www.pewforum.org.

[6] Ibid.

twenties, she's returned to the small town where she grew up, where she lives with her twin sister. Her childhood experience of religion was one of an occasionally confusing variety. "My grandparents were Presbyterians, and my parents were Pentecostal," she says. "Early morning was serious service with recitation and everyone was in their sixties; then we'd go to the vibrant church with waving hands and the spirit empowering the body." Cassandra also grew up surrounded by Mormons, so she also had some exposure to Mormon theology. This diversity of experiences got Cassandra interested in the idea that Christianity doesn't have to mean one single thing from a young age. "The great thing I learned was that Christianity had a lot of variety," she says. "I learned about gifts and learned my intellectuality was my gift."

Cassandra attended a historically Christian college that is now "mostly secular," and it was there that she began her inquiries into the roots of the Christian faith she'd been raised in. Although she had a wide range of choices to draw from in terms of choosing a religious path, her time in college became the beginning of her separation from participating in religion. "In college I ended up in an evangelical group, and at the same time took Hebrew classes, and I was in a class with this wonderful gruff archeologist and three Jewish students—all from different [Jewish] denominations. Each of them came with their biases, and I came with mine, and our biases showed in our translations." But Cassandra's growing engagement in studying the Hebrew scriptures was met with skepticism by her evangelical friends. "My evangelical group would say those classes were dangerous and my mind couldn't do both." Faced with making a decision, Cassandra chose the path that she'd earlier been taught was a gift: her intellectuality. "I went with the group that made more sense," she says. "That was my professors. The raising of hands was feeling superficial."

The schism between Cassandra's intellectual pursuits and her evangelical fellowship mirrored the split between her Mainline grandparents and her Pentecostal parents. But in Cassandra's case, the more she learned about theology as an intellectual practice, the less she felt a pull to participate in organized religion. "So gradually, my intellectual activities replaced my need for church.

I became uncomfortable there." Finally, she stood up at one of the evangelical group's final meetings and told them not to be afraid to ask questions and learn the history of their religion. "It's good and makes things more meaningful and deeper," she told her group, "and I knew that wasn't welcome. No one shut me down, but I'd been corrected before." She realized it was time to move on. But, as it turned out, she had moved on for good. "After that I never went to church again. Once in a while I go, but for interest's sake. I read and discuss the texts and then I go once," she says, "and it's enough."

After college and graduate school, Cassandra wound up teaching abroad in Japan and then received a grant to go to Great Britain to study interfaith relations—a topic she continued to be interested in after her own upbringing and cultural clashes over religion in college. In those two countries she was exposed to a greater cultural secularism than she'd experienced in America, which led to further questions about the role of religion in society. Because Great Britain technically has a national religion, which the United States does not, "they have a more structured conversation about religion than we do because the government can sanction it. They have some contentious debates about being Christian, real public, formal debate that's government sanctioned." Cassandra says that her time in Japan and England showed her that while she didn't like the Christian fundamentalist response to secularism, she also worries that "secularism is ignoring the spiritual dimension of human life. I want to protect people I respect, like [religious scholar] Elaine Pagels, who have had powerful spiritual experiences that are legitimate. My experiences [of religion] are mostly intellectual but still important to me." After her experiences abroad she felt that it was "too harsh to go only to secularism. When everyone gets so nervous about religion," she says, "we forget this other side that's empowering and beautiful and profound." She worries that "the United States seems to be going that way and people don't realize it. Young people don't have the background to see it, and older people can't communicate it." Cassandra works for a scholarly religious institute and mentions that she's working with a number of older scholars of religion. "The reason my job is fulfilling," she says, "is because I'm talking to seventy and eighty year olds" about the differences between secularism and religion. The older generation, she thinks, has a stronger understanding of how to navigate those differences.

When I ask, in light of her gut feeling that pure secularism isn't right, if Cassandra is done with churchgoing for good, she admits that the problem is that she feels she can't find the right church. "I feel I'm also forgetting that side of religion," the side that provides the "empowering and beautiful and profound" contrast to secularism she mentioned earlier, "because I'm not participating." She does "shop around" but never goes back to the same church more than a few times. "Almost always it's because the ministers piss me off." As a scholar of religion she finds most sermons are "grossly inaccurate historically. Unitarians are often too broad. I don't want to pretend I don't have a Christian background," she says. "Catholics do it well, get you closer to a spiritual feeling." But she struggles with Mainline Protestant churches. "The more casual they are, the harder time they have doing it. They're trying to be friendly. I'm looking for a feeling of connection to something larger than myself."

But in spite of her struggles with organized religion, Cassandra does feel a strong sense of what she identifies as God. She mentions she's been reading the work of the writer Wendell Berry, who often writes about "connecting with community and land." "God to me means collective reality, what powers our existence," she says. "It's not personal, it's connection. A lot of [churches] I go to don't achieve that." That search for a collective sense of God has become more meaningful to her since she and her twin sister became the adoptive parents of two kids. Of her search for a true sense of finding God through community, she says, "We're trying to give this to our kids. And I have no way to communicate that feeling to our kids because it always comes packaged with other stuff I don't agree with."

Many religions' emphasis on "sexuality stuff" is off-putting to Cassandra's sense of how God works. "Who cares? It's a cultural thing, not about ethics. So what if they did it one way in biblical times? It's silly to nitpick." Although she's not "a hardline socially liberal anything, but I always lean left"; on the issue of bias against LGBTQ people, she believes churches have taken "interesting and deep religion [and made] it petty." She tried attending a United Church of Christ church in a nearby town and found its members "making jokes about supporting Obama. I don't want to talk about politics" when it comes to religion. Then logistical problems arise from her choice to live in a rural area. "The closest church that did good liturgy is fifty miles away. I'm not going to drive fifty miles on Sunday," she admits. The sense that honoring community matters more in terms of finding God trumps a long commute every week. When Sunday morning arrives, "I'm going to pick my kids' community over driving to a church."

Those same kids ran in and out of the room while we talked, with Cassandra taking breaks to tell them where a toy had gone or where a snack could be found. They are a brother and sister, five and six years old, and it's an open adoption. Cassandra and her twin sister co-adopted them, and they live together as a family. "We've focused on the fact that we were raised in a rural area," she says, and after living all over the world, she and her sister bought a house in the town where they grew up to raise the new family, start a small farm, and "focus on the rural because that's easier for us to do." When I ask her to say more about her growing interest in Wendell Berry's ideas about community and the land, she talks about the connections between becoming a parent and building a community from the ground up. "We became foster parents because we wanted to do something local, to really go local and be ethically doing something right here, to help people. When you really try to change things, you change things and your whole life changes too." What began as a foster-parent situation turned into an adoptive parent one fairly quickly. "We could only do it once because the family needed us permanently," she says. "So I suppose that's a secular way of thinking; in this life I'm trying to do the right thing with the people right in front of me. I didn't expect it to go this route, and it was hard for me. I thought it was temporary, and it proved not to be. It made me let go of ideas about who I was, and when two little people look at you and say, no one else said yes, you've got to do it." Of her life before becoming a parent, Cassandra says, "I was pretty selfish and now I do things for the kids." Parenting, she adds, has a spiritual side as well. Too many contemporary spiritual movements, according to Cassandra, prioritize "individualistic talk and identity movements. That seems petty when you're trying to take care of a family and community."

"The reason I became a foster parent is because there was a group of people right here that needed help and I was gonna do it," she asserts. "And it created a community. How do you join a community? You show up and keep doing something until people expect and hope you'll be there. You fill a need and keep filling it until you become part of the fabric. It turned out we became a permanent fixture in the life of one family." She adds that an open adoption might not be the ideal for some people, but that things don't always happen the way people want them to. Take what arrives and who arrives, she says, "otherwise it's selfish. You have to be open to who's needed. One of the best pieces of advice I heard was that I had to become the parent my kids needed instead of the parent I wanted to be. It's a loss in some ways, but I gained a lot too. So identity politics forget that we belong to each other." Cassandra and her sister have created ties in the ethnic community their kids come from, but they also work hard to teach the kids about the value of homesteading and gardening, with a consideration for ethics that reaches far beyond the range of what a church might be able to provide. And while Cassandra has chosen to prioritize a different kind of community than the one she experienced in her own versions of religion, she has also experienced a real sense of conversion to a way of caring for others church never provided her with, and one that secular culture, in her experience, tends to neglect. "Our lives have become unique because of how things ended up," she says, "but we didn't plan it that way."

Toward the end of our conversation, with a lively kid on the other end piping up and asking for her attention, I ask her if she thinks she's moved beyond her upbringing in two different versions of Christianity. "What I don't want is to be antagonistic toward Christians," she says. "I still identify with Christianity very strongly. I'm Christian but not religious." Cassandra and her sister have been reading the work of the Vietnamese Buddhist monk Thich

Nhat Hanh, and using "tools from Buddhism to supplement our Christian knowledge." Thich Nhat Hanh's work on using meditation as a way of channeling anger proved especially helpful in her early days as an adoptive parent. "Adoption is emotional, and I wasn't expecting that direction but I morally couldn't refuse it," she says. "Buddhism helped me be where I was. I don't want to be a Buddhist, but meditation makes more sense that prayer does. I like the feeling of prayer, reaching out, but I'm reaching out to everything around me." She says that she doesn't feel connected to Buddhist stories historically or culturally, instead feeling connected to Christian stories. She adds that she and her sister are not becoming Buddhists, but that Buddhism is helping them navigate a transitional time in their lives. After a life of transitions, between Christian faiths, around the world as a student and teacher, into a career in theology and scholarship, and now into parenthood, homesteading, and a real sense of building deep ties and community with the help of a faraway Asian-born monk, Cassandra has come home.

Liminal space, as it turns out, can be spiritually fruitful. Shortly after we spoke, Carolyn took up a prayer practice over Lent, trying a different form of prayer for a week at a time, and writing about each in a blog. Her atheist boyfriend supported the project but chose not to participate; however, Carolyn wrote, "given that my exact beliefs are still being worked out (will they ever not be?), I think my praying alone was, at least for this time in my life, an asset." She may not have drilled down into one single faith, and perhaps she never will, but that doesn't mean she lacks faith altogether. She has plenty.

And faith sometimes grows out of community rather than prayer. Cassandra's description of the power of community and what it means to become a parent to people who need her calls back to descriptions of early Christian communities, when there was no such thing as an institutional church but believers still clustered together, cared for one another, worked together, put bread on the table, and ate it.

Somewhere outside of the regulations and inherent divisions of expecting people to choose a single religion, there are people like this, people who will spend a lifetime moving between faiths, or, perhaps, creating their own. Some will be alone in the journey, and others will find ways to share it with others. Maybe this undefined, mixed, blended, self-invented religion won't meet in a church or a synagogue, or have a congregation, or a single sacred scripture. Instead, perhaps it will look like a mostly nonbelieving family watching a child move through a religious ritual; or like a woman sitting alone at prayer, finding her way toward God; or like a new kind of family, eating the food it has grown.

4

When Women Don't Worship

When my first nonfiction book was released in 2009, the marketing department at my former publisher encouraged me to get on Twitter, which was becoming increasingly popular as a book-promoting tool. Already overwhelmed by having to maintain a blog, keep up a Facebook page, and do interviews and readings, I sent out a few desultory Tweets to my two dozen followers and promptly gave up. But, encouraged once again by a different publisher's marketing department, when my next book came out, I slowly wound up engaging in some worthwhile Twitter conversations with a group of religion writers, theologians, bloggers, and journalists. One Mother's Day, while I was reading Elizabeth Johnson's landmark book of feminist theology *She Who Is*, I sent out what I thought was a pretty innocuous, slightly sassy tweet: "By the way, God's not a dude."

What proceeded from there encapsulated the vast reasons why women abandon organized religion. Lots of women and a few men retweeted what I thought was a harmless and funny message, but even more people got upset. I was called an idiot, a dyke, a '70s feminist, and a heretic, among other things, and one particularly persistent person demanded to know which diocese I belonged to so that he could report me to the local bishop. In the following years, after every essay I wrote that appeared in a Catholic magazine, and even in secular ones, I was sent blisteringly angry letters, emails, and messages through Facebook and Twitter, even if the topic of my work seemed harmless. When I wrote about visiting an Episcopal church, a blogger picked up the essay and went on a tirade about how "pathetic" it was to expect that women should be able to participate in religion beyond sitting in a pew. That blog went viral. It's easy to imagine what happened next: more vitriol, in heavy doses.

Whenever this depressingly regular turn of events occurred, there was some consolation in the fact that the same thing was happening to renowned theologians and women religious like Elizabeth Johnson, Sandra Schneiders, Margaret Farley, and to my fellow female religion writers, but the anger lobbed toward any woman who dared to write about religion became exhausting to witness. Just by speaking up, we became targets. Even if we were experts on a topic, we were told we were wrong about it. When this pushed me to think about leaving Catholicism, my spiritual director, a religious sister who'd been through her own share of frustration, told me that I had to stay put because at least I was able to write, even if it put me on the receiving end of rage. But as female friends streamed out of Catholicism, or wept with frustration about the latest censure of the LCWR (Leadership Conference of Women Religious), or gritted their teeth through an insulting homily, the questions about what it meant to be female and religious became increasingly difficult to answer.

In 1987 Elizabeth Johnson became the first female faculty member to get to a tenure review at the Catholic University of America. Although she was already a well-respected theologian, former Cardinal Ratzinger (later Pope Benedict XVI) took the "extraordinary measure" of having Johnson interrogated by every cardinal in the United States in order to get approval for an article she'd written from the Congregation for the Doctrine of the Faith (CDF). "There were these men, and they had all the power," Johnson told writer Jamie Manson years later. "I was vulnerable and at their mercy. I kept thinking that in another century, they would be lighting the fires outside."[1] But Johnson survived that interrogation, only to have the United States Conference of Catholic Bishops issue a public critique of her widely respected book *Quest for the Living God* years later. After more than fifty

---

[1] Jamie L. Manson, "Feminism in Faith: Sister Elizabeth Johnson's Challenge to the Vatican," *BuzzFeed,* March 6, 2014.

years as a woman religious, Johnson made the decision to stay in the church. To those outside of Catholicism, this may seem to defy logic. However, as Johnson told Manson, "If you feel deeply enough, you stay. Not because you're a masochist, but because it's worth it. You're struggling for the soul of something."[2]

It's easy to see why women could feel that staying within religions that don't offer them an equal voice is tantamount to choosing a life of struggle. Over the course of interviewing people for this book, I spoke to dozens of women who had abandoned Catholicism, Islam, Orthodox Judaism, Southern Baptist, and Seventh-day Adventist churches—and many other faiths that do not ordain women. But even within denominations that have female clergy, there is still a lifetime of difficulty ahead. Years ago a female Episcopal priest told me that once women were ordained in the Anglican communion, discussions of feminism ended. The assumption from the mostly male hierarchy was that ordination was enough; the work was done. When the Church of England voted to approve female bishops in July 2014, a female friend in Episcopal seminary said she was pleased but admitted that gender equality was still a work in progress in the Church of England. A female rabbi I met talked of the ongoing struggles in Israel with the Women of the Wall, a group of activists in Israel fighting to pray in *tallit, tefellin,* and *kippah,* as men do. With all of the obstacles in the way of women attaining an equal position in organized religion, it is understandable why so many younger women are abandoning it. Some choose instead to be Nones, and some choose to be loyal dissidents, attending services but questioning and fighting patriarchal structures in religion.

In 2008 Barry Kosmin and Ariela Keysar of Trinity College in Connecticut conducted a survey of American religion. Of the 54,461 people they surveyed, one in five self-identified as atheist, agnostic, or religiously unaffiliated. The authors grouped these respondents together as "Nones." Sixty percent of the Nones surveyed were male. According to the authors, "The ratio of sixty males to forty females is a remarkable result. These

---

[2] Ibid.

gender patterns correspond with many earlier findings that show women to be more religious than men, particularly in majority Christian societies."[3] Empirical evidence for this is not difficult to find. Certainly, the majority of people attending almost every Christian parish is female. Women made up the majority in every religion Kosmin and Keysar surveyed with the exception of "Eastern Religions" (grouped together) and Islam, both of which had a fractional male majority. Other surveys I skimmed offered similar results. In each, women made up a smaller percentage of the religiously unaffiliated than men. As I discovered over the course of my interviews, many women have stories of being hurt by organized religion, which may be why some of them are less public about their lack of religious affiliation. When it comes to leaving religion, family ties run deep, as do social and cultural ones, making many women's nonbelief an issue of deep secrecy. Women leave religion for any number of reasons. But one thing many of them have in common is a history of pain.

Sarah works in communications at a nonprofit working to uphold the separation of church and state in America. We spoke the week the Supreme Court granted an exemption to the Hobby Lobby chain in providing birth control to its employees in a landmark case about religious freedom. The devout Christian family that owns the Hobby Lobby stores contended that health plans requiring them to cover contraception for their employees were a violation of their religious beliefs, which led to their suing the US Department of Health. This led to a prolonged national debate over whether or not for-profit corporations have the right to the freedom of religion promised in the Constitution. Understandably, as she'd worked on the campaign against Hobby Lobby, Sarah's phone was ringing off the hook, and she was swamped with emails

---

[3] Barry A. Kosmin and Ariela Keysar, "American Religious Identification Survey Summary Report," Trinity College, March 1, 2009, http://b27.cc.trincoll.edu.

and messages on social media. Her busy week was added to by the fact that she had been profiled in a national newspaper column the previous weekend. In that column, for the first time, she had publicly opened up about her experiences of depression and sexual assault while attending a Christian college. At the Baptist-run Cedarville College, Creationism is taught as factual, students are required to take Bible study courses, and the school's culture is fundamentalist. This environment discouraged her from reporting her sexual assault and led to the beginning of her realization that she no longer believed in God. She tried to force belief in God but ultimately failed.

I ask Sarah about the time between realizing she no longer believed in God and her decision to tell people she'd become an atheist. "It was confusing, because it was easier to acknowledge I didn't want to be a fundamentalist than saying I didn't have faith in Christianity any longer," she says. While still a student, Sarah "tried to transition to a more liberal and feminist Christianity, but I still didn't believe in God. It was difficult to leave a deity behind altogether. I had Buddhist and Pagan friends and went along to their rituals. I called myself an agnostic for a while because it was easier than calling myself an atheist." Like many people brought up in strict religious homes, Sarah clung to the idea that she might be able to hold on to some of the good things about religion, including her relationships with her family and friends; she had led an isolated life, being separated from secular culture, and her ties to the fundamentalist community were hard to unravel. But eventually the discomfort with her circumstances at Cedarville pushed her into telling people what had changed. She no longer believed in God.

Because Sarah works for a nonprofit that advocates for the separation of church and state and has so recently been involved in debates about the Hobby Lobby case, I ask her what it's like being a female public figure for the atheist movement. One misconception many people share, she admits, is that atheists are anti-religion. "Although I'm an atheist," she says, "I'm not anti-religion, and I'm critical of hardline atheists because they don't understand the longing for the spiritual." As a result, her "biggest criticism comes from other atheists," who would prefer that she be more openly critical of believers. Thanks to the public personas of Richard

Dawkins, Sam Harris, and the late Christopher Hitchens, the mental image many people have of atheists is of angry middle-aged white guys. Sarah is twenty-six-year-old woman from a deeply religious background; she defies expectations.

We talk about the sexism that seems to be an issue in the atheist community. "I've had so many debates with myself trying to figure this out," she says. Part of the root problem is that "atheism is still white male dominated, and there's a lot of privilege at play. A lot of women and people of color are still religious, and you have to acknowledge that." She also mentions a disproportionate overlap in behavior between public atheists and the Religious Right. Her own background in fundamentalism complicates matters as well. "Being an ex-fundamentalist," she says, "a lot of people [who become atheists] are angry and don't move away from that fundamentalist script. They're using the same tactics, but different terms." From early on, however, Sarah's atheism became an intrinsic part of her feminism. Her master's degree was an examination of evangelical aid groups, "and I was very critical of them because of an extension of colonialism." That led to work in women's rights, which is part of her current job. The experiences she had at Cedarville were difficult to speak about publicly; however, she now sees telling that story as part of her work, so that "people can learn how this affects women and LGBTQ people."

We talk for a bit about the differences between Sarah's atheism, with its focus on women's rights, and the previous generation's atheism. "New atheists . . . are more willing to interact with people of faith. Social circles are more diverse, and we have friends of different backgrounds." This is a demographic shift, she thinks, that is similar to what's happening in organized religion, with younger people being exposed to a wider range of religious and nonreligious traditions from early on. And it echoes the views of other young atheists I spoke to. Having come from a tightly knit fundamentalist community, however, the loss of that community has had an impact on Sarah's relationships with her family and childhood friends.

When I ask if she's found a way to be part of a nonreligious community, "that's been difficult," she admits. "I haven't found a community in atheism. I've found it to be fairly hostile. But I have found a community among ex-fundamentalists. It's so insular, and when you come into the mainstream world if you have a support network, it's much easier. So I tend to gravitate to those people more than anything else." Among others who, like her, moved out of fundamentalism, "no matter their religion, the bonding transcends. That's what frustrates me about organized atheism," she adds. "It's supposed to be about your lack of belief in God all the time. It seems there are a lot more important issues to be discussed." She understands some of the "prickliness" of atheists, who are subject to the stigma of their willingness to identify as nonbelievers. However, as we wrap up our conversation, she adds, "I have a lot of hope for people talking about the need for a healthier community, interfaith work, how we can support each other and have less focus on the lack of belief in God." She wants to focus instead on "building relationships with people from different backgrounds." Of the future of women in atheism, Sarah simply says, "I'm hoping."

Beyond openly atheist women like Sarah, in the larger community of doubters and seekers there are also a number of women who are still attached to a religious community. But these skeptical believers come to a life of faith with a different set of issues than men do. Mothers, whether single or married, face complexities about parenting that sometimes make dealing with a masculine church hierarchy difficult to tolerate.

Mary Ann and I have interacted for many months on social media, and when we speak, I know that she has been working her way back into church attendance after some time away. She's currently somewhere between describing herself as unaffiliated and describing herself as a believer. Much of her life has been about navigating what it means to come from a religious childhood. Her father was a minister in the United Church of Canada, a Mainline Protestant denomination. Being a "clergy kid" shaped Mary Ann's childhood. "Dad was always challenging me to think through theology," she says, "and Mom, who dropped out of seminary to marry my dad, was very much the intuitive feeling religion thinker." Along with the intellectual and intuitive ways of looking at faith that she got from her parents, Mary Ann grew up with her father "asking tough questions of faith" and encouraging her to do the same. She was taught to pick apart Old Testament stories and have difficult conversations about religion. Like many Boomer parents, Mary Ann's parents allowed her to feel her way into religion rather than forcing her into it. But that changed when she went to high school.

"I was a wicked teenager, or so my parents thought," she says. As a result, Mary Ann was sent off to a boarding school in Canada that was affiliated with the Community of Jesus, an ultra-traditional Episcopal church in Massachusetts. For someone raised in a form of religious life where she was allowed to ask questions, the transition to the boarding school's "incredibly strict" way of life was painful. "I can still tell you how the days were structured to the minute," she says. "Girls didn't wear pants without a reason. Specific social events dictated when you could wear pants." Harder than the dress code to adjust to was the idea that you couldn't be critical of how religion was taught. "I'd gone from this family where we do question to this place where we don't," Mary Ann adds. "Those two years were a real challenge for me. I did a lot of hiding and thinking and not talking."

Another shift at boarding school was her first encounter with sexism cloaked under the guise of tradition. All prayer was based on an older form of the Book of Common Prayer with "no modern language." And "boys were separated from girls. Girls had to be modest because boys are stupid." Mary Ann was suddenly encountering "all of that kind of culture blaming women." This extended to the first lecture the school gave students. They attended in pajamas, but "our housecoats had to be floor length, even though the boys never saw them. The headmaster would come in and talk about modesty. As a teenager you don't put those things together. Later, you think it was kind of creepy and inappropriate." The school tried to squash her independent and questioning spirit, and this led to conflicts with the administration and teachers that were exacerbated by the emphasis on girls being subjected to rules that were different from boys' rules. For all of the frustrations she encountered in those years, however, Mary Ann now says, "That experience did later help me to form my arguments for feminism and egalitarianism."

When Mary Ann went off to university, she had a brief, youthful engagement, and when that broke off, she became engaged again. "The second guy I was engaged to identified as Hindu and Buddhist," she says, "so there was an opportunity to explore what that looked like and to skip church. And over the course of that time I did some exploring on my own." Because she didn't want to accept someone else's tradition, she looked into Paganism and Wicca and "didn't feel it contravened anything in my previous world," although she admits that it would have freaked out her mother. After that engagement broke off, she moved to Vermont to spend time with her grandparents and take charge of their caretaking, and "going to church was part of what we did." When she returned to the university, Mary Ann joined an Anglican church choir and was reconnected with a major part of her childhood experience of religion. "I knew who Bach was before I knew anybody else," she says. "We had two pianos in the house, and there was always music of some kind." She earned two degrees in music and one in psychology, and music became the tether that allowed her to reconnect with Christianity. Looking back on that today, she says, "As I'm struggling now with the liturgy and patriarchy, music is keeping me there."

Mary Ann continued to attend Anglican churches after university, but was thrust into church politics at one parish that led to complicated issues with a rector who pushed her away. "At that point," she says, "I was married, and my now ex has two kids from his first marriage." In light of her battles with the rector and the new relationship, "we took a year off church." After that year the family tried again at a different parish, where Mary Ann got involved with youth leadership and running youth groups. "We hardly went to service," she says, "but we were in the basement" with the kids. Although she was beginning to form lifelong bonds with the kids from that parish, her marriage was starting to disintegrate. "I was recognizing it was an abusive relationship," she says, preferring not to describe what that entailed. "So when I took a break from the church" to deal with the breakdown of the marriage and the outcomes of the abuse, "there was really no outreach. So I stopped going to church at that point. It felt very disconnected. I stopped going and received nothing."

Singing and music eventually pulled Mary Ann back into church life again. And that led her to an interesting turn in her life. "In the interim" between her divorce and starting to sing in a church choir again, "I went back to school in theology. It's been an interesting road going back after eighteen years. Part of my healing process was to recognize that my ex-husband called me stupid and downplayed my intelligence, so going back to school was terrifying." Returning to academia, she says, was part of the process of "trying to decide if I was smart enough." Mary Ann works for a food bank, which in Canada is government funded. She sees the "very simple work of feeding people" as part of "how I could live my faith without having to do so in a broadcasting manner. I get to do work that's important and helps me maintain my morals and principles without having to say 'look at me—I'm a Christian.'" Pursuing a theology degree, however, "is about me in a broader sense, which is nice." When I ask if she's going for an MDiv, which would enable her to work for a parish or pursue ordination, she says no. "I want an academic master's. I've done enough service."

Although Mary Ann has been feeling her way back into religion through music at her Anglican parish, a major obstacle remains. "The wording of the liturgy is so antiquated and masculine," she says. "We're accustomed to it." However, "at the same time, those liturgies can be really hurtful to people for whom male relationships were not comfortable." Years ago, when Mary Ann was leading a confirmation class of eight and nine-year-olds, "we had the kids rewrite the Lord's Prayer in their own words. One of the girls didn't have a father. He'd never been part of her life. She had no male role models. We put it in historical context. She understood all of that. But she said, 'Why do I have to pray that way now?'" For Mary Ann and the kids she worked with, the "language of father and son can be difficult. It can push people away instead of being welcoming. It was intended to be welcoming and humanizing," as originally written, but given the social changes and different under-standing about gender roles we live with now, "it isn't at this point."

Like many Christian women Mary Ann "accepted patriarchal language for a long time because it was historical. We're a people of history. But I'm realizing that's not enough." When I ask how she deals with the inner conflict over these masculine images of God, she says, "I change the language in the prayers. It doesn't always work. I think about ways the liturgy could be changed to be poetic and historical but still egalitarian." The gender of Jesus is not an issue for her. "The reality is that Christ was a man because he was born in first-century Palestine. That doesn't bother me. But the fact that he treated women as humans and the church treats them as second class is troubling."

Mary Ann's son is six years old, and "he's part of the conver-sation" she has about what religion means in her life. About the ongoing conflicts she feels over the way Christianity deals with women, "my faith itself isn't the question. It's the expression of it. I don't want to take that away from my child. I'm showing him the world around him." Her own experiences of moving in and out of religion, she hopes, will lead her son to a broader kind of understanding of the choices ahead of him when it comes to his own faith. Mary Ann says, "I'm hoping there's a healthy balance of broader spirituality mixed in with specific religions" in his fu-ture. But he does already show one sign of being aware of practical ways in which religion can become a form of social change. Like his mother, he gives away food to people in the neighborhood. So, Mary Ann says, "he takes after his mommy."

Women from religions that still have arranged marriages can face hard choices about faith when those marriages fall apart. Mary Ann and Shujana come from different parts of the world and different faith traditions. Their reasons for distancing themselves from religion are not the same, yet they overlap and demonstrate how women can be alienated from the faiths and cultures that promised to nurture and guide them when those religions' intentions and actions become misaligned.

Shujana's family comes from Pakistan; it immigrated to the United States in the late 1960s. "They're Sunni Muslims," she says, a branch of Islam, the world's second-largest religion after Christianity. Shujana's family reflects Sunni Islam's tendency toward a more orthodox form of Islamic practice. Of the branches of her family she says that some are "super orthodox and others less so. My mom's was more orthodox; women cover their faces and wear burkas. My mother was actually the first in her family tree to not wear burka. Her brothers sent her off to university and she got a BA and MA." Of her father's side she says, "In general my dad's family is pretty orthodox and conservative. And they espouse a more political Islam."

Shujana was born and raised in a large East Coast city. Religion permeated her childhood home. "My parents raised us with religion as part of our lives," she says. After decades in America "my mother's gotten more and more conservative over the years. Now I'd consider her too rigid. Sometimes I struggle with that," she admits. She describes her parents' political sensibility as "quite open" and says that her mother is pro choice (many Muslims accept abortion as permissible up to the fourth month of pregnancy, according to the Hadith, the collection of prophetic traditions), but religiously conservative. For Shujana, that religious conservatism "was tough for me growing up." At an early age she wanted to pick apart the ideas behind the faith she was being taught. "I remember asking myself questions growing up about why people around me would go to hell, why would Martin Luther King go to hell." In Islamic Jahannam, or hell, nearly all Christians would be condemned, much in the same way that many Christian concepts of hell condemn non-Christians. "Those are questions I asked as a child," Shujana says. That inquisitiveness and doubt about some teachings she was being exposed to began to bother Shujana more and more as she matured. "I tried to ignore those questions growing up," she says. But the questions didn't stop.

As she grew older, Shujana's questioning began to distance her from the Islamic idea of God. "I think that after a certain point I couldn't ignore those questions because I was espousing something I didn't believe in," she says. "I think I felt a little irresponsible in terms of favoring your own community, that sense of tribalism, it made me uncomfortable." She describes this as putting one's own tribe first, "that relies on a certain 'othering' of people that growing up in a multicultural society makes impossible." However, she acknowledges that this was something her parents brought with them to America, and it "was relevant to their society and culture." But for Shujana, her questioning created a gap between their way of thinking and her own. She says she's still very connected to her community and accepted but also admits that many members of that community tell her she should "just be more religious." Taking a stand about her doubts has meant that she has experienced a sense of isolation, even if there is still acceptance. "If you don't believe in those things it can come at a price. One of the things I experienced was loss of some connections. I'm not as in contact with my family as much as I used to be." She pauses for a moment. "I wish that were different." Of her current life, she says, "I think I'm at the point of not being able to ignore those questions now. If I'd lived differently, I think I would have been capable of ignoring those questions my whole life. There's a lot of security in community and family." But a series of events lead to a breaking point in Shujana's ability to live her faith life in the way her family wanted her to.

"The pivotal point for me was I had been married at twenty-nine. It was a semi-arranged situation," she says. "The gist is that I didn't know this gentleman as well as I should have. I felt very pressured to go through a courtship that didn't suit me." The marriage took a toll on Shujana. "I paid a heavy price" for agreeing to it, "because I was in an unhappy and abusive marriage. If I'd had the time and space to go through a proper courtship and dating I would never have married him. There would have been signs, and I would have caught onto them." She adds that during that time "I made choices that were not very good choices, and if I'd had the freedom to choose, I'd have never chosen this man." After the breakup of the relationship, she made the decision to live alone and gave herself "permission to have space." In that space she encountered her doubts head on. "One afternoon I said I'd let my mind go, there were some questions I couldn't ignore. Once I was alone I'd explore them and let my mind be free. I let go of everything." Some years later she is still experiencing the aftermath. Of the marriage and its effect on her belief she says, "I feel I'm going through a deconstruction process."

Being willing to have freedom of mind was a difficult transition for her, because, as she was brought up, "I equated free thought with being godless." However, she adds, "I think I felt intuitively that I had the right to ask these questions and get to the bottom of what had happened." Her time alone is one that she describes as "wanting to take off those masks you always wear," because she wanted to "be myself in public space for the first time, and it was terrifying, because I always felt like I had to represent my culture and religion." She goes on to say that the time after her marriage fell apart meant "dealing with myself in a continuous manner" for the first time, away from the orthodoxy she had been part of for so long. Shujana's doubts and questions, however, led to an unexpected revelation: "The thing I discovered is that God was on this side of it as well. If God exists on this side of the questions then what was all of this stuff? Was I being lied to and, if so, why?"

She pauses and backtracks to explain. "I have to admit to having resentments," she adds. "I was tightly controlled my whole life. On some level I want to remain in contact" with family and the Muslim community, "but on another, I just don't connect with them spiritually. I want to just remain respectful." However, she continues to hold on to her new idea of God. And her God is now a God of independence. "What I believe wouldn't be considered Islam by orthodox believers," she says. "I think that some Muslims would identify me as an apostate. But digging deep with those questions gave me a lot of confidence. It was okay for me to make these decisions because God is still here and I can be myself and don't have to be answerable to anybody but myself."

Of her religious identity today, Shujana says, "I identify as Muslim because culturally I was raised in a Muslim household. My household has a Muslim appearance. It's unmistakable." But she knows that from the outside, her willingness to be vocal about her doubts can be challenging to other Muslims. "People say I'm culturally Muslim and that's fine," she says. "I identify as a spiritual person." Her present relationship with Islam is one in which she is willing to accept that her faith is a deep part of her identity even if she is unsure about it. "Raised Muslim, I learned to call God Allah, and I'm fine with that. God is God, and different words are different. I still believe in the prophet Muhammad and that he was a wise man." However, she adds, "I'm not an observant Muslim, and my mother says I take way too much pride in that. I wish she understood."

One factor in Shujana's current wrestling with her Islamic identity is her deeply entrenched commitment to feminism. "I'm a diehard feminist," she says. Balancing that with having been brought up in a patriarchal religion can cause static. "I think it's hard for me" to be both in and out of Islam, "because I have these core feminist beliefs, and I'd taken women's studies 101, and that's a lot of books." Of her decision to agree to an arranged marriage, she says, "I've been schooled pretty hard core, and one of the things about having beliefs and having that view and then making the choices I was making, there's a really big contrast. That troubled me because I didn't feel responsible; I felt I was just following a herd in my politics." And she sometimes struggles with the point of view of other Muslims, especially when it leads to the sort of tribalism she mentioned earlier. "I have troubles with some of the less multicultural perspectives of some Muslims, the racism, things like that are not being concerned about the politics of other people or religions. The homophobia of Muslims really bugs me."

But more recently she has begun to reach a compromise point with her faith life. "I try to approach the mosque in a fresh way," she says. "I'm starting to find that there are a few people who are very open and observant. I feel like those friendships are more important." For the first time she has begun to find peers who are both progressive and active practitioners of Islam, "people I genuinely want to see. Before I just associated with people because I had to." This has led to more open relationships with religious leaders as well. "At this point I'm in the process of talking to my imam about a talk he gave that went all sorts of wrong, and he's open to that. I plan to go in there and just be myself." She's open with one of the female directors of that mosque about living with her current boyfriend without being married to him, and that leader "is happy and supports me, and it's empowering. These people don't condemn or judge me." After the painful experience of her marriage and the distancing from family that came as a result, Shujana is determined to make a space in Islam for a more feminist perspective. "I feel like I've broken ground for myself, and I hope other women can do the same," she says. "Religious spaces aren't always safe spaces for women, and I want to make that better, at least in mosque."

If Shujana is correct that religious spaces aren't always safe for women, that means that women will continually be tested in their affiliations with religions that have entrenched histories of sexism. To belong to a faith in which God is called only by male names or where men continue to hold authoritarian roles, or where women are considered inferior to men means that women are often silenced. With silence comes marginalization. For Sarah, Mary Ann, and Shujana, that marginalization also means encountering hard questions about a God who would create humanity in God's image and somehow determine that the female segment of humanity is inferior. For all three of these women those questions led to distance and even to separation—from religion, from community, and from God.

In Arabic, the word *islam* means "submission," something these women were each asked to do. Sarah submitted herself to the fundamentalist beliefs of her family. Mary Ann submitted herself to a difficult marriage, as did Shujana. And each of them broke out of that submission in her own way. But they each emerged into a new kind of belief, whether it was religious or secular. They each found, in the fracturing of old identities, something lasting. Rather than finding a God created in the image of man, they found themselves.

5

Queering the Nones

Statistics reveal only a sliver of what it means to be human. They are a useful tool, but they are only a tool. And when it comes to writing about members of the LGBTQ community, because our understanding of human sexuality is evolving and changing even as I write this sentence, beginning with a series of percentages about how many LGBTQ people have left religion or have been marginalized by it would reduce them to a collection of questions and answers tossed out by data collectors, in surveys that are often conducted in haste. Just as there are many ways to be in religion, on the fringes of religion, or out of religion, there is no one way for LGBTQ people to believe or not to believe. Statistics are a framework; human beings are three dimensional and stunning in their diversity.

I begin this chapter with a few caveats. First, as a straight person, my positioning must be taken into consideration. While many of my friends and the people I interviewed for this book run the gamut of the LGBTQ spectrum, at best I can consider myself to be in solidarity with them, but I cannot speak about their experience as an insider, nor will I attempt to; my task, when writing about them, is to step back and let them speak for themselves. Second, on the advice of many people I spoke to in and outside of theology, academia, and community organizing, I am going to use the term *queer* in an attempt to be more inclusive. Patrick Cheng, a theologian and Episcopal priest, explains the preference for this term in his own theology in *Radical Love:*

There is a second meaning of "queer" that is an intentional reclaiming of a word that previously had only negative connotations. In recent years, the word "queer" has been used by many LGBT people as a positive label that proudly embraces all that is transgressive or opposed to societal norms, particularly with respect to sexuality and gender identity.[1]

Old Catholic Church priest and writer Shay Kearns too uses the word *queer.* "I feel comfortable with this word. It fits my identity. It fits how I understand my community."[2]

To be queer has always meant that one exists, from the outside view, on the fringes of religion. In the Abrahamic faiths scripture castigates same-sex relationships, with consequences the people I spoke to deal with every day. Hinduism and Buddhism have more complex views of queer relationships; according to Nancy Bonvillain, in Hinduism "homosexuality is regarded as one of the possible expressions of human desire."[3] Although Buddhism has long looked down on some same-sex sexual practices, especially for monks and nuns, the Dalai Lama said in 2014 that as a Buddhist he supported marriage equality: "If two people—a couple—feel that way is really more practical, more sort of satisfaction, both sides fully agree, then OK." However, he added, "People should still follow their own religion's rules on sexuality"[4]

In queer theology there has been an ongoing effort to recast the "clobber passages" of the Bible (for example, the "sin of Sodom" is really about the Sodomites' lack of hospitality to outsiders, not about anal sex; the Leviticus purity code was based, at best, on very primitive pseudoscience; the injunctions in Romans, Corinthians, and Timothy are often based on mistranslations and misreadings

---

[1] Patrick S. Cheng, *Radical Love: An Introduction to Queer Theology* (New York: Seabury Books, 2011), 5.

[2] Fr. Shay Kearns, "Why I Use the Word 'Queer,'" Camp Osiris, http://www.camposiris.com/queer/.

[3] Nancy Bonvillain, *Women and Men: Cultural Constructs of Gender,* 3rd ed. (Upper Saddle River, NJ: Prentice Hall, 2001), 281.

[4] AFP, "Dalai Lama Supports Gay Marriage," *The Telegraph,* March 7, 2014.

of the original Greek and were most likely not written by Paul, and so on). But that effort comes very late in the game when we're looking at the more than two thousand years of entrenched homophobia that has been an unfortunate characteristic of Western religion. Although there have always been queer people present in every culture, society has often done its best to make their lives difficult. The astonishingly rapid change in the way many Americans view same-sex marriage may seem like a sign that the lives of those in the queer community are getting easier, but it doesn't take more than a cursory skim through the news to discover that hate crimes, threats of violence, stereotyping, depression, suicide, rejection, workplace discrimination, and religious discrimination are everyday occurrences.

So why do queer people drift from religion? The obvious answer is that for the most part, religion does not make room for them to live their lives fully. The Catholic Church, notwithstanding Pope Francis's "who am I to judge?"[5] declaration about gay priests, still states in *The Catechism of the Catholic Church* that homosexuality is "objectively disordered" and "a trial."[6] The Southern Baptist Convention issued a resolution in 1996 that "even a desire to engage in a homosexual relationship is always sinful, impure, degrading, shameful, unnatural, indecent and perverted."[7] Although moderate and progressive Muslims argue that interpretations of the Qur'an that forbid homosexual acts are erroneous, the death penalty is still in place for queer people in some Islamic-majority countries, including Saudi Arabia, Iran, Afghanistan, Mauritania, and Sudan. Orthodox Judaism refuses to ordain openly gay rabbis. For many queer believers, given the circumstances they live in, the fact remains that, based on organized religion, God can seem cruel, distant, absent, or indifferent. But God can also be present to them outside of institutional religions

---

[5] Rachel Donadio, "On Gay Priests, Pope Francis Asks, 'Who Am I to Judge?,'" *New York Times,* July 29, 2013.

[6] "Chastity and Homosexuality," in *The Catechism of the Catholic Church*, 2nd ed. (Vatican: Libreria Editrice Vaticana, 2012), 625–26.

[7] "Stances of Faiths on LGBT Issues: Southern Baptist Convention," Human Rights Campaign, http://www.hrc.org.

in ways that religions might not be able to recognize. Faith, like grace, often occurs on the margins.

Dave contacted me through Twitter after he'd attended a panel talk I had given on doubt and faith in writing at the Associated Writing Programs conference. He told me he'd been working on a long essay about his own process of discerning the role of faith in his life, and I offered to take a look at it, which led to our having a long conversation a few months later. Like many writers, Dave speaks thoughtfully, pausing often to expand on a thought, and his frankness about his struggles with faith comes through both in his writing and during our conversation. Now in his mid-twenties Dave's early experiences of religion were deeply embedded in his childhood and adolescent psyche. "I grew up in religion and even pursued it fervently in college," he says. Today, however, he has stepped back from the evangelical faith that surrounded him and is building a kind of belief that feels more self-constructed and self-defined. "I'm realizing more and more that while I still identify as a Christian believer," he says, "my sense of that far more resembles the unaffiliated friends of mine than it does the active Christian identification than I see elsewhere." For Dave, that represents a radical shift from the "take it or leave it" sense of faith that he grew up with. "While I maybe was able to vocalize this need to analyze my faith," while growing up, "there was always this conversation about 'you've inherited these beliefs, but one day you have to claim them as your own.'" Analysis and questioning, so important to the life Dave now lives, were alien to his childhood experience of religion.

Dave grew up in Idaho, the son of a Pentecostal Assemblies of God minister. His father ministered in a "small, rural church" from the time Dave was five until he was seventeen. Dave attended a Christian school, and like many minister's kids, he found himself absorbed in church culture. Although he's distanced himself from his Pentecostal past, he does admit now that a kind of joy was present in that part of his life. Like many Christian kids born in the 1980s and 1990s, he also immersed himself in Christian pop culture, which was proliferating. "I ate it up," he says. "I collected Christian pop music and radio dramas, subscribed to *Relevant* magazine. I was very into it, and it seemed very natural, and I had a reputation as the golden child in those years, because not only was I able to do everything right but I seemed to enjoy doing it." Underneath Dave's life as a minister's kid, however, a challenge was beginning to arise. Looking back, he says, "I was also, deep under the surface, wrestling with my sexuality and how that fit or how to extract it." And the experience of living in that take it or leave it version of Christian faith ultimately led to struggles a few years after he left for college. Once he'd exited the bubble of his childhood, Dave "was forced into finally having to analyze and reconcile what it was I was actually believing and doing, and that became a difficult and dark time. Because I'd never asked questions before, and I didn't like it."

Dave's parents supported his decision to attend a secular college. At the end of high school he "went to pick up my final and my history professor asked where I was looking to go to college. I said I'd been looking at schools" in the rural area where he grew up, "and she said no, no, no, you should look outside the state." Dave wound up at a college where he "found the creative writing program and fit right in." He also immersed himself in campus ministry, working for a Presbyterian program. The first year was fine "because I had no other responsibilities," but sophomore year, burnout began to seem like a present danger. "I'd been invited to lead a Bible study and play music, and I had a part-time job, and that year was horrendous," he says. "I probably said yes to ten too many things. That may have been where some of my questions started." Friction with the Bible study leader, in addition to issues with the ministry's leadership, led Dave to step back from campus-ministry work. However, as soon as college ended, he spent a year in a Presbyterian internship program. "Maybe I went into that unwisely, because I was already getting pretty burnt out on ministry things. When I think about it, I'd been in the ministry since I was five, because of my father's participation. I was always helping out, even as a little boy." By the time Dave began the internship, he'd been ministering for twenty years. "I went into the internship with a victory lap mindset," he says, and he did enjoy the people he worked with, "but ministry is a very stressful and lonely experience if you're not partnered," he adds. "All the other interns had significant others they could vent and let off steam with," but Dave was single, and, in retrospect, "the isolated feeling drove me to really consider the analysis and coming to faith on my own that I'd been putting off for so long."

The beginning of Dave's period of questioning the faith he'd been brought up in was partially also triggered by his discovering two books: Dostoyevsky's *The Brothers Karamazov* and Kathleen Norris's *The Cloister Walk.* "Both of those books were formative and eye opening. There were two competing themes of my faith up until that time: the legalism and moralism that stems from the inerrancy of scripture I was raised to believe, and then in college the discussion was about vocation and the work God's called you to do." But the vocation discussions Dave heard in college were primarily about either going into ministry or working at a nonprofit. "I realize now that books are my vocation, and book people are my church. They enrich my life and I feel like I've been called to serve them." But that was not presented as an option when the issue of vocation came up.

As to the struggle over having been taught that the Bible is inerrant, Dave felt "liberated when I started to think of the Bible as an object, as a commodity in the way it's delivered to us. It was printed by machines, typed and printed by people, that leaves space for me to wonder about the people translating and selling this book." His ideas about Christ also began to shift. Now, he says, "I can think of Jesus as the Word of God and see the book as kind of a snapshot, but I wouldn't want to confuse the two, the snapshot for the real thing." As Dave passed through his "crucible year of interning" and wrestled with these doubts and questions for the first time, "it's not the making my faith my own my parents would have hoped for," but having been "kept to the isolation of my thoughts and frustrations" during his internship, "this is what I've been left with."

After Dave left his internship, he took another year to process his new perspective before he was ready to come out as a gay man. He moved to a Pacific Northwest city with a friend from the ministry. "We were in similar places," Dave says. "He's wrestled with agnostic ambiguity." Dave and his friend spent a lot of time talking over their struggles and doubts and eventually found their way to what had been one of the first racially integrated churches in his city, a Presbyterian parish. "It was a perfect place for us to go because they were feeling the need for grace. Grace is such a big part of what I've begun to realize is absolutely necessary," Dave says. "Because I'd done everything on the right terms and context growing up, I didn't get grace."

Discovering an "open and affirming church" was something Dave needed to experience. "I had a church phobia," he says, "because I didn't want to be asked to participate in anything, not even coffee hour. But going there and getting to meet several gay Christians started to help me realize that possibility as well." The first gay Christian Dave had ever heard of "who hadn't been shamed out of the church" was Episcopal Bishop Gene Robinson, but Dave says that his awareness of Robinson from the perspective of his hometown in Idaho was "more about the stigma that he bore." The new parish offered something different. "So these were the first gay Christians I was meeting firsthand and talking with. I think that . . . threads were coming together." Dave briefly dated a woman that year, "a trial run that didn't go well," but as he began to see a new possibility of living openly in his sexuality, life, along with his perspective on faith, began to change. "Because I could step away, in a new city where I'd been introduced to the possibility of out, well-adjusted, gay Christians, that's when I started the coming-out process. It was a charmed experience." His parents demonstrated some pushback but were eventually supportive, and his friend was there to support him and was "happy to see me stepping fully into how I am." As he says in retrospect, "Coming out was very much a result of where I had found myself after asking myself some very critical questions about faith. It was not the other way around. It wasn't asking questions and then finding space for being a gay Christian. It's so counter to the narrative I was fed about homosexuality and what happens when people come out and leave the church. It was always that order of things. For me, it was very much reversed."

Today, Dave looks at religion from a mostly outside point of view. "I've been with my boyfriend two years. We're living together and it's glorious," but neither he nor his boyfriend feels any sense of urgency to commit to becoming part of a church. He describes his attendance at churches as "peripheral" and "occasional," but there's no sense of loss in his voice when he says it. "My boyfriend isn't religious, but we enjoy the compline service at an Episcopal church. I've actually always been surprised when he suggests it. He went to church when he was very small, and then his mom died when he was really young, and [his family's] aversion to religion now has a lot to do with how insensitive the church members were with the 'she's in a better place' platitudes." The compline services offer a kind of middle way. "Because of the hands-off approach to a compline service, for me it's the least I can do with church. Going at 9 p.m. on a Sunday, listening to a choir, and leaving. It satisfies a spiritual thirst for both of us in different capacities."

Dave may have moved to an in-between space that looks very little like the church of his upbringing, but in that space what he has found looks to him like grace. "I'm so thankful I'm not experiencing so many stark changes. I always am wondering if this is the right path, but not in a defeatist sort of way. It's just sort of a curiosity. That describes my faith the best. It's uncertain, and I'm in a good place with all of that." While that kind of statement may seem lacking in commitment, Dave is moving toward something deeper. His continued commitment to being a Christian and to building a relationship with God, even outside of a parish, is "why grace is so important to me. If I needed grace even when I was doing everything right, the distance between my relationship with God then and now on the grand scale is a very small shift when it comes to the necessity of grace." And of the importance of the life, death, and resurrection of Jesus, Dave says, "I believe it's for everyone and the whole world and it's big enough to encompass everything from doubt to certainty. And I think it's a bigger, more defined faith than I could have ever thought I could possess as a teenager. I do very much feel like this faith, no matter how atheistic or agnostic from the outside, is very much my own, and I wouldn't have it any other way."

For a gay man like Dave, the decision to participate, or not, in a religion that doesn't recognize his sexuality as natural is, perhaps, a stark one. But for many straight people who consider themselves to be in solidarity with the queer community, institutional religions' treatment of their queer family and friends can also push them away from being a regular participant in a church community. One of the root words that led to the English word *religion* is the Latin *ligare,* one meaning of which is "to bind." So for those bound both to a queer community through the webs of family and friendship and to a religion that condemns or alienates members of that community, life is full of tension, and they may enter the same liminal space that becomes the dwelling ground for many Nones.

Nicole was raised in a Seventh-day Adventist family in the Pacific Northwest. Her maternal grandfather was an Adventist pastor, so her mother is "third or fourth generation" Adventist. Her father converted to Adventism when he married Nicole's mother, "so he's always been Adventist to me." From the beginning of her life Nicole was immersed in Adventism and attended Adventist schools all the way through college. Adventism worldwide has about 18 million members,[8] and the Adventist church runs nearly eight thousand schools, including fourteen colleges in the United States.[9] When I remark to Nicole that I've seen Adventist churches but have never met an Adventist, she says that although the religion is large, its members tend to socialize within Adventist

---

[8] "Seventh-day Adventist World Church Statistics 2012," The Official Site of the Seventh-Day Adventist World Church, http://www.adventist.org/.

[9] "Colleges and Universities," Adventist Colleges and Universities, http://www.adventistcolleges.org.

communities and don't always mix with people from outside the religion. So Nicole grew up culturally apart, although she was not aware of it until later, when her burgeoning feminism and work with young gay men newly diagnosed as HIV positive led to her departure from the religion that had shaped much of her early life.

Adventists were in the minority in the liberal-leaning area where Nicole grew up. "Oddly enough, I didn't feel set apart at the time because everyone I knew was Adventist." Nicole's family was "really active," and she taught Vacation Bible School and Sabbath School. Like Jews, Adventists celebrate Sabbath on Saturday, and that means "no TV, no going out to eat." The Adventist Sabbath is "kind of a family day," and Nicole's family strictly adhered to its observance. But from early on there was a push and pull between Nicole's growing awareness of social issues and the very conservative perspective of the Adventist Church. "Even though my parents were active, they're both very liberal in terms of politics. I think that was a piece that didn't reconcile." Although she remembers her Adventist childhood as "a happy way to grow up" and an enjoyable experience of being part of a tight-knit community, that very emphasis on building and sustaining a community eventually revealed layers of hypocrisy to Nicole. "In a lot of ways the values I learned growing up are what led me away from the church."

Adventism places an emphasis on female modesty in dress that was difficult for Nicole to understand as a child. "At the school there was no jewelry allowed, and the older generation was extremely conservative and not welcoming to visitors. I brought a friend to church one day who was not Adventist, and one of the elders scolded her for wearing earrings. There was that ugly piece. There was a stricter generation than I was growing up with." The generation gap and the prejudices it occasionally espoused felt starkly different. "My parents were always clear about the nonjudgment piece and politically accepting all people." But this became an area of confusion for her, because it embodied a kind of inherent contradiction. "The politics I was exposed to in the home were not matching up from things I was seeing from a lot of people in the church."

Nicole's shift away from Adventism began as soon as she arrived at college. Church attendance was required of all students, but, Nicole says, she became "less regular" in her attendance. "Even though it was an Adventist college, I was in psychology, and my major was pretty liberal in that context." And attending an Adventist college was not really a matter of choice: "I was against going to an Adventist college, but my parents insisted." Today, "that's a huge piece of my resentment, because I have massive student loans and have to pay monthly to a discriminatory institution." She started to identify more strongly as a feminist and queer ally in her college years, prompted in part by the realization that "Adventism was founded by a woman," the nineteenth-century Christian visionary and writer Ellen White. "So it seemed 'off' that women couldn't be ordained. That was crazy to me."

Nicole began to move toward her current career in social work, and as she took courses to prepare, she "became passionate about institutional discrimination wherever it exists. Church, employers, laws. And the values my parents taught me and that I learned through the church were anti-discrimination." Today, she's not sure if she believes in God or not, but she emphasizes that the God she grew up with "wouldn't be discriminatory or hateful." An essay assignment to analyze homosexuality in the Bible also led her, for the first time, to "really look into the few passages explicitly about that, and look at the language and context," from which she determined that the Bible's references to homosexuality are not about "consensual relationships" but about "war crime or rape." Adventists believe in the inerrancy of scripture, so Nicole's creeping sense of skepticism about her church's teachings on women and queer people began to grow greater. "I was thinking about having kids myself, and if I would raise them in the church, and what I would teach them." She decided that there was no way she wanted to raise children in a discriminatory faith. In her junior year Nicole wrote a letter to the Adventist hierarchy and asked to be officially removed from the religion.

Around the same time Nicole began an internship at an AIDS foundation that brought her into San Francisco a couple of days a week. She'd heard about Buddhism in a world religions class, and being close to the Bay Area, she took advantage of the local interest in Buddhism and visited the San Francisco Zen Center's Green Gulch Farm. "I was going through a breakup and heard about a meditation class at the LGBT center in San Francisco. I started going and practicing meditation." She also began studying yoga, and slowly Buddhist thinking began to take the place of the Christian religion she'd grown up in. Some traces of her Adventist upbringing color her experiences of Buddhism. "I still keep the Sabbath in my own way, so having the dharma talk on Saturday felt natural to me."

"What I love about Buddhism is that it's a practice and a lifestyle and not a religion as it applies in my life," Nicole says. "When you grow up in a faith that's very strict, it's all or none; questioning things and having doubts isn't openly accepted; you have to believe it in exactly that way." She adds that she has a hard time "getting on board" with the biblical picture of Jesus and instead tends to see him as a historical figure. "And there's this fear piece. Your salvation is based on what you believe about the afterlife. So with Buddhism it was just a practice and a way to live," one that also fit into the values of community she was raised with. "Mindfulness can be Sabbath, being a day apart. A lot of things were actually parallel to me. It seemed more flexible and some of the magical thinking about Christianity that I can't quite buy into wasn't as present in Buddhism." Nicole says that she did consider seeking a different Christian church at one time, but that "at that point there didn't seem to be any Christian religions open to accepting and marrying gay people. So, that ruled out all the Christians." Today, Nicole works with women and young gay men newly diagnosed as HIV positive. Her decision to leave a religion that rejects those young men is one of solidarity. "This is a matter of life and death. All of them have contemplated suicide, and it's usually around religion."

Nicole recently relocated to a new city, and she admits that she is having a hard time feeling connected to others in a spiritual sense. "Community is really important, and I've struggled with how I would create that for my own kids if I have them. Religion is a natural way to find that, and if you don't have it, you have to look for other ways." She is part of a yoga community, though not a Buddhist one, but admits that it's not the same as being around "people who've known you your whole life. My two best girlfriends from childhood, one is still Adventist. But I do sense a little bit of isolation as an adult compared to how I grow up. I think it's important to create that if I have children. And I am also feeling a little isolated from my family. They're very accepting, but I'm sure they'd prefer if I were still Adventist."

Nonetheless, Nicole is clear that she's not going back. This has led to some disconnect from her mother, an "educated, intelligent woman" who "works with a lot of young kids struggling with their sexuality, but she justifies staying in the church by trying to create change from within. And that's great," Nicole says, but it's not for her. She struggles with the idea that her mother "truly believes Jonah was swallowed by the whale" and denies evolution. "Some of that has created isolation for me," and she and her mother are not as close as they once were as a result. "I see a lot of peers who don't participate at all" in religion, Nicole says, but she adds that having some sort of spiritual practice is important to her. "I think churches will change." But Nicole, for one, is not willing to wait around for that. "People just don't buy into the anti-gay thing," she says. If the Adventist faith of her childhood denies the fullness of queer life and love, that's enough to cause Nicole to disconnect permanently.

Nonetheless, she sees signs of optimism about acceptance and equality in her peer group. Of the past social and religious prejudices against queer people, Nicole says, "That's changing already." But most of those changes are occurring outside of religion.

For Dave, Nicole, and others who see the damage religion has done to many queer people, it's understandable that many members of the generations that have embraced and supported queer equality by large margins would come to the decision that participating in religion means participating in prejudice. And by that logic, it is clear why so many of them are leaving institutional religion. Even a believer like Dave finds that religion is only workable in small doses; it is easier, for him, to practice it outside of institutional walls, within a self-created framework.

While some denominations ordain openly queer clergy and bless same-sex unions, they are few and far between. Many other religions send what amounts to a schizophrenic message: You are loved, unless you act on your desire; if you act on it, you are condemned. Faced with that kind of double talk, it is no wonder that queer people and those who love them struggle to feel that there is any real place to belong, and to be true to themselves, within institutionalized religion. And until that changes, for many it is easier to be a None.

6

Among the Catholics

Years before I began this book, I wrote a different one: a book about being Catholic. Or rather, about becoming Catholic; I was not yet confident enough to wear that as a label in spite of the fact that I'd been culturally Catholic since the moment of my conception, educated in Catholic schools all the way through my MFA, and Catholic in the stuff I wrote since I was able to move a pen. But just as I was about to go out on a book tour and meet people who had perhaps read this book (or would perhaps want to buy a copy), I stopped believing in God. Or rather, believing in God became difficult. So I signed up for a retreat that guaranteed me two sessions of spiritual direction a week for three weeks. My hope was that someone would be able to hammer God back into my consciousness.

The guy I met with, who would later become a Jesuit priest and my friend in reverse order, was small and muscular, with a shaved head and a beard. He looked rather like a compact pirate. And as is my wont as a person whose life is crammed to the limit with activity and duty, I got straight to the point. "I'm suffering from a severe case of doubt," I told the Jesuit pirate. In short, I demanded a manifest God. Point me to evidence. So he tried the Jesuit thing: "Imagine yourself in a scene from the Bible; okay, let's try this woman who touches the tassel of Jesus' cloak because she wants to be healed from those bad periods she's had forever. She's not suffering from doubt." So we talked through the scene. "And what does she do when she gets home?" he asked. "She does the laundry," I replied. Pragmatism, while useful, is not conducive to spiritual awakening.

After a few weeks of struggling through this, the pirate finally shrugged his shoulders. "You know," he said. "I can't cure your doubt." But he was willing to give me a solid piece of advice, one which I still cling to, years later. "If we didn't have doubt," he said, "we wouldn't be human."

Astute readers may by now have noticed a rather large demographic absent from this book thus far. Where, you may well ask, are the Catholics? Don't lapsed Catholics represent 13 percent of Americans?[1] Isn't Catholicism losing its younger people? Where are they going? And why are they going?

So many people who responded to my queries were Catholic that Catholic Nones, reverts, and those who remain on the margins of the religion constitute most of the latter half of this book. And as my own doubts and questions nudged me further away from a firm identification as a Catholic and into something more like a doubter who occasionally turned up at mass, my conversations with lapsed, ex, part-time, and skeptical Catholics revealed the same reasons for stepping back or out that had been bothering me since my own return to the church seven years ago: the top-down hierarchy, the lack of gender parity, the often callous attitude toward the queer community, and remote or uncaring priests. But something else was present in many of these conversations, something I suspected that Catholic Nones, doubters, and searchers will grapple with for the rest of our lives. The term a friend used to describe the work of the lapsed Catholic playwright Stephen Adly Guirgis is useful here. People who were once Catholic are "God haunted."

In the spring of 2014 four researchers published the results of a multi-year study of young Catholics under the title *Young*

---

[1] "America's Changing Religious Landscape: Christians Decline Sharply as Share of Population; Unaffiliated and Other Faiths Continue to Grow," PEW Research Center, May 12, 2015, http://www.pewforum.org.

Catholics Today: Emerging Adults In, Out of, and Gone from the Church."[2] They reported, perhaps unsurprisingly, that young Catholics may be just as spiritually at sea as many of their religiously unaffiliated peers, a story of "decline and loss."

Young Catholics Today attempts to explore some of the reasons behind that decline. Much of the first section of the book is focused on the role parents play in giving their children a Catholic identity, and the authors conclude that many parents of Millennials were "poorly formed in Catholic faith and life." The reasons for this are manifold, but the authors point to a long era of "institutional weakening" of the church.

The ripple effect of this on the formation of a Catholic identity in younger adults is traced throughout the book, with chapters examining the role of Catholic high schools, religious trajectories from youth into adulthood, and the ways in which Catholic identity affects a person's life outcome. The authors also offer an excursus on what it means to be Catholic today—an open-ended question, to be sure, but one that these young adults are clearly grappling with.

It is not a spoiler to say that the book's conclusions about the future of young adults in Catholicism are fairly grim. One need only look around at the average Sunday mass to see that young adults are few and far between. The study offers some correctives to commonly held assumptions many people have about what helps in the formation of a Catholic identity. For example, attending a Catholic high school does not increase a person's odds of staying in the church. Lapsed Catholics are highly likely to remain lapsed for a lifetime, whereas lapsed Protestants are not. The majority of Catholic youth, like most youth, have premarital sex and use birth control. And they are sorely lacking in role models. In fact, the study finds that teens and young adults find mass more

---

[2] Christian Smith, Kyle Longest, Jonathan Hill, and Kari Christoffersen, *Young Catholics Today: Emerging Adults In, Out of, and Gone from the Church* (New York: Oxford University Press, 2014). The study that provided the data for the book is the National Study of Youth and Religion, directed by Christian Smith (University of Notre Dame) and Lisa Pearce (University of North Carolina at Chapel Hill). The research study began in 2001 and is funded through 2015.

rewarding if they can socialize with "important adults" in their church communities.

So what does it mean to be Catholic today if so many younger Catholics don't go to mass, don't participate in social activities with other Catholics, don't agree with the Vatican on issues of birth control and same-sex marriage, and are uncomfortable identifying as Catholic among their peers? Are they still Catholic, and who gets to say that they are? Based on the evidence, we could easily assume the church is headed for a future of nothing but decline: empty parishes, a massive priest shortage, a hemorrhaging of its lifeblood in the young.

Some would argue with this, and point to the evidence of a renewed interest in traditional Catholicism among younger Catholics. Their embrace of practices like Eucharistic Adoration, the Liturgy of the Hours, and Latin mass could be an indication that they find grounding in practicing a very structured version of the faith. And there are statistics showing that in terms of vocations, signs of growth may be present among orders of women religious that wear habits or choose a cloistered form of life. However, in the case of these communities, "whatever these institutes are doing is unlikely to offset losses in the tens of thousands elsewhere." And a few of these recently founded traditionalist communities "flourished initially and then tailed off."[3] In other words, while traditional Catholicism appeals to some younger Catholics, it's unclear exactly where this movement is going, how many people are involved, and what its future looks like. But traditionalist Catholics can hardly be considered Nones, nor do they really fit in with the seeker identity of their marginally Catholic or lapsed Catholic peers. The Catholicism they embrace is one of answers, not questions. The return to tradition, some of them feel, is what will help them to avoid getting lost in the questions and slipping away from their faith.

---

[3] David Gibson, "Declining Number of US Nuns, Even in Traditional Orders, Charted in New Study," Religion News Service, October 13, 2014. The study was published by the Center for Applied Research in the Apostolate (CARA) at Georgetown University.

The people I interviewed don't resemble the Catholics described above. They are still Catholic, but in many ways they are Catholic Nones. They wear their Catholicism loosely, or, in some cases, it follows them through life like a ghost. They form intentional Catholic communities but don't participate in mass. They go into seminaries doubting that there even is a God. They like Pope Francis but struggle with the bishops. They drop everything to join monasteries but still cling to their ties in the secular world. They try other religions and find themselves alienated. They attempt to return to the church but bring with them all of the doubts and questions that had driven them out in the first place. If this muddled, messy kind of faith is an impending sign of resurrection, it is like the one depicted in the Gospels: confusing, conflicted, and based on a series of accounts from prophetic voices of the people no one wanted to listen to or to believe.

I met the monk, before he was a monk, on Facebook. The message icon flickered to life when an actor we both know made the connection: two writers, two creative people, two weirdos, two Catholics. Perhaps we'd like to get acquainted? The monk back then had a different name; let's call him Anthony, the desert father, the first monk. I went into the cafe where he worked, a busy spot near the school where I teach, and introduced myself. We were both members of the vanishing demographic of thirty- and forty-somethings in our respective parishes, both taller than average, both of us crazy for Baroque music and difficult books, both of us, back then, just finding our way into a life of faith. I had returned from a twenty-year lapse; he'd just been baptized. We were, back then, new arrivals to this messy thing called religion.

Anthony's parish was shrinking. Even at the Easter Vigil its pews were half full. But he had wandered in during his search for a church at a time when he could barely articulate the thing that was pulling him into religion. Religion hadn't been a particularly pressing issue during his childhood and had played almost no part in his adult life up until then. A charismatic pastor and a small but fiercely loyal congregation made it easy to go, week after week, to ask questions and have them answered, to begin the Rite of Christian Initiation of Adults (RCIA), to be the single person baptized at the Easter Vigil. As an actor, he was used to having lights on his face; his parish rents a humming spotlight at Easter and shines it onto the baptismal pool. One Catholic is wrapped in a white garment, and the entire church applauds him.

Even at the beginning of his walk, thoughts about vocation filtered through Anthony's consciousness. He read Mary Doria Russell's *The Sparrow* and considered becoming a Jesuit; he got to know some of the local Dominicans and took my husband and me to a Christmas concert at their priory. Then one year a Benedictine began attending Anthony's parish; we were eating Chinese food together when Anthony told me he was thinking about meeting the Benedictine vocation director.

I have friends who are priests. We text, we tweet, we go out for cocktails and eat enchiladas and see movies. They have iPhones and laptops and live in community, but they do not live away from the world. Like me, they are always in it. Like me, they are able to choose when they come and go. Anthony will not be able to leave the monastery for a full year during his novitiate. His time on the computer is limited, and using the phone is difficult. The closest city is an hour's drive. Needless to say, he doesn't have a cell phone.

But before he was a novice, Anthony went off to the monastery as a candidate. He left his job and packed up his apartment, and I drove to pick him and his remaining belongings up: three boxes and a backpack. The rest had been given away. On his final night outside the monastery, we sat in front of my laptop and looked at pictures of where he was going. He'd been on several vocational retreats; now the rubber would meet the road. Each part of the monastery had a story he could already tell. The characters behind the austere looking faces of the Benedictines came to life in my friend's voice. The next day I drove him to the train station, and for three months he entered that life.

Benedictines give candidates a month's break before they enter the novitiate. So Anthony came back. I picked him up once again at the train station and found my friend dazed after hours of travel. The daze lasted for several days. He'd vanish into the room I use as an office every couple of hours, his breviary shoved into a pocket. I'd forgotten about the Liturgy of the Hours, the seven sets of prayers that monastics have used to punctuate their days for centuries. In fact, I could barely recall which one was compline and which one was lauds. One night I overheard him talking with my husband in the kitchen: "So what exactly are vows?" asked the guy I'd married, sincerely curious to find out. And my friend explained poverty, chastity, stability, and obedience as I eaves-dropped from the living room.

Anthony's visit gave me the first chance I'd had to chew over my religious weakening with someone at length. But as the days went by and we talked about God and the church, one thing that had always been present in our friendship became clearer. I was jealous of my friend's faith. He admitted to struggles in the mon-astery; he missed the freedom of the secular world and tried to hang on to his connections with it, but no matter what happened, God's existence was rarely in doubt. I recalled what Matthew, the former rabbinical candidate turned atheist had said about a "God-shaped hole" in his life. My own God-shaped hole looked like the absence of the thing that came so easily to my friend: the willingness to trust that he was beloved, that he was directed, that God was moving in his life.

Midway through writing this manuscript I flew to Kentucky to spend two weeks teaching a course in spiritual autobiography to graduate students in an ecumenical master's program. Half of my students were from the Presbyterian seminary in Louisville. The remainder was a mixed bag including lay Catholics, one semi-retired priest, an ex-Presbyterian newly converted to the Episco-pal Church, a Lutheran dance choreographer who'd grown up a Jehovah's Witness, and a gay Baptist minister who'd broken off from the Southern Baptist Convention when he started agitating for marriage equality in Kentucky. The professor who'd hired me found that the cheapest and closest housing was in the Mother-house of the Ursuline Sisters of Louisville. The order's foundress, Saint Angela Merici, had in the 1500s imagined a radical idea: a religious community of women who would live among the poor people they served rather than being enclosed in convents, and who wouldn't wear habits. Unsurprisingly, the church hierarchy wasn't happy with this, and Ursulines were eventually ordered into convents and habits, where they stayed until Vatican II a few hundred years later, at which point they happily went back to civvies and living among the poor. The Motherhouse was the retirement home for the sisters who could no longer live on their own. The oldest in their community was 103; a 100–year-old sister still attended mass every day, shuffling up and down the hallways with a walker.

Spending two weeks living with women religious who are best described as feisty and challenging while spending my afternoons teaching a thoughtful group of people how to write their own spiritual stories forced me to consider this God issue at length. And one afternoon, the theologian who had invited me to come teach drove me out to the monastery of Gethsemani, best known as the home of Thomas Merton, one of my favorite writers, himself a model of a lifelong searcher in spite of his decision to live as an enclosed Trappist. Brother Paul Quenon, who'd been one of Merton's novices, took us on a long hike around the monastery grounds, and then we had dinner at Merton's hermitage with Brother Paul and another Trappist.

While Brother Paul was cooking, he invited me to poke around the hermitage, just a few small rooms clustered together and furnished with stuff that looks like it came from a yard sale. I stuck my head into the chapel, its yellowish walls of painted brick, and inhaled the wood-smoke smell that pervaded the tiny house. "The last guy who visited was a Franciscan priest," Brother Paul informed me from the kitchen. "He went into the chapel on his knees." My doubts made me worry about crossing its threshold, but the Trappists encouraged me to step in. Wondering for a moment if I was capable of a grand gesture, I decided the best I could do would be to touch the altar with a finger. For the person stuck in doubt, grand gestures may indeed be out of range.

The Gospel Reading that day had been the story of Jesus walking on water. While we sat on the porch and drank sour red wine, the theologian who'd brought me to Gethsemani asked the Trappists what they made of that story. If Peter initially manages to stay afloat, why does he suddenly sink? Brother Paul had some thoughts. "When Peter got into the water," he said, "he already had doubt." In other words, don't wade in if you're not sure, or you may sink.

My students wrote exquisitely about their own struggles with God and faith, but they all seemed to land on the side of belief. And talking about religion in a mixed group of Christians was occasionally fraught with explosions I wasn't adequately prepared to prevent. The Presbyterians and Baptists and Lutherans didn't know much about Catholicism, and I'd assigned three books by Catholic writers, requiring lots of conversation and explication about sacraments and rituals and Vatican II and saints, the stuff Catholics take for granted that often strains the credulity of our fellow Christians. We were discussing Dorothy Day's *The Long Loneliness* when the newly converted Episcopalian in the class blurted out, "Why was Dorothy Day Catholic anyway? She seems so progressive, but I couldn't belong to a church that was so terrible to women and LGBT people. Why go somewhere where your friends can't take communion?" There was one of those pauses that every teacher dreads, the gut-churning silence that indicates someone's said something so touchy that nobody wants to pipe up in response. But the gay Baptist came to my rescue. "Even if a church doesn't love you," he said in his caramel-coated accent, "some part of you still loves it. Loves it. So you stay."

Like many Catholics, my love for the church is innate. My family is buried in Catholic graveyards, we went to Catholic schools, and like every other Irish Catholic family in America, we had a dusty photograph of our martyrs RFK and JFK in silhouette hanging in the kitchen. As a post–Vatican II Catholic, however, it wasn't the "smells and bells" that kept pulling me back, but the social justice lean of my parish community, the courage of women religious, the relentless messages of a loving God who waits patiently for us. Instinct is a powerful draw when it comes to religion. Gay Chicano Catholic writer Richard Rodriguez talks about this stubborn draw to a religion that was not always friendly to him in an interview with Bill Moyers in 2006.

I never think of my religion as being something that I choose. I think in some ways, it's something that . . . it chooses me. I mean, people have asked me for many years, you know, "How can you be a Catholic when you're also a gay man?" Well, like, how could I not be a Catholic? It's not something that I choose. It's chosen me. It feels larger than me. It feels like, you know, they're asking me how can you be your parents' son? It's nothing that I chose. It's something that I believe in. It encompasses me.[4]

However, like many liberal-leaning Catholics, my instinct is always to add a "but" to the statement "I'm a Catholic." As a person who lives most of her life in the secular world, my Catholicism is often defined by what I don't believe rather than what I do. And it was clear that any faith in God that could be as easily fractured as mine was not, after all, a very strong faith.

Catholics have likely struggled with doubt over God's existence since Jesus left his mortal form in favor of one that was less about the body. Once I heard a priest say in a homily on the feast of the Ascension that he never knew what to do with this moment in the Gospels; it was like we were being abandoned en masse. We celebrate the fact that God in human form decided not to dwell among us for very long. *Acedia* is probably the closest term we have for the kind of spiritual torpor that Christians have written about since the first hermits went into the desert in search of God and found instead that they were praying to something that rarely, if ever, responded. Saint John Cassian wrote about this liminal state in the fourth century:

He [the monk] looks about anxiously this way and that, and sighs that none of the brethren come to see him, and often goes in and out of his cell, and frequently gazes up at the sun, as if it was too slow in setting, and so a kind of

---

[4]"Bill Moyers on Faith and Reason: Richard Rodriguez," PBS, July 21, 2006.

unreasonable confusion of mind takes possession of him like some foul darkness.[5]

Saint John Cassian called this the noonday demon, an apathetic restlessness, a search that went nowhere, an extended period of what some refer to as "dry prayer." Acedia settled into the lives of many saints and holy people and remained parked there, in some cases, for the greater part of a lifetime. Probably its most famous modern manifestation is in Mother Teresa, who lived in a state of religious crisis for the better part of four decades. In a letter to one of her spiritual confidantes she wrote of prayer that "as for me, the silence and emptiness is so great that I look and do not see, listen and do not hear."[6] Mother Teresa filled this God-shaped hole with hard work, self-inflicted physical pain through mortifications of the flesh, and hours of prayer and eucharistic adoration that brought her no consolation. Acedia is loneliness, sadness, distance from God. And the longer it goes on, the less some people feel it is worth the bother of occupying a place in the church.

The church also offers few options for resolving acedia. Dry prayer is prescribed a dosage of more prayer by spiritual directors and priests. Doubt about God? Spend more time in church, maybe work with the poor, but also to keep turning up at mass. And spend more time praying. Are you restless and feeling caged by your faith? Try praying. Again. Or perhaps you should go on a silent retreat, which is nightmarish when the Noonday Demon is at your back. Anyone who's experienced acedia knows that prayer in this state is torturous and that spending days in silence around the kind of pious people who most often go on retreats is the worst possible place to put yourself. What Cassian referred to as "an unreasonable confusion of mind" means that the extended concentration of prayer is impossible; the Buddhists refer to this as a "monkey mind," one that leaps from one idea to the other,

---

[5] John Cassian, *Institutes* X:2.

[6] David Van Biema, "Mother Teresa's Crisis of Faith," *Time Magazine* (August 23, 2007).

never able to settle on a central thing. So telling those in a state of acedia that they should simply pray their way back into believing is tantamount to telling a depressed person to look on the bright side. In many ways, it's insulting.

Doubt is a passage every believer will go through. For some, it will last decades. For others, it will cycle through their lives like a chronic illness, exacerbated by circumstance or soothed by community, listening, an honest response to questions, and care. For many, it ends in a final decision that God is not real. Doubt, for some, is a movement through fire, a season in the wilderness, a grinding sense of isolation and separation from something that feels consoling and soothing. For those who have lost it, that consolation is what we might think of as belief. When I think of my friend the monk, I know he experiences torpor, loneliness, and isolation, but I also know he experiences the presence of God with some sort of regularity, or else he would have never have been drawn to a religious life in the first place. But doubt must exist somewhere in his days, perhaps when the Noonday Demon comes knocking, as it always will. Doubt may be lonely, and it may be isolating, but it is also inevitable. Perhaps Catholics who know the doubt of the disciples—who waited for the resurrection of a God they weren't sure existed any more—might begin to understand that doubt might be something else.

Catholic faith, compared to many other Christian expressions of faith, is more elaborate, more embellished with a panoply of sacraments, feast days, holy days, rituals, and rites. We have more saints, more churches, more books of theology, more religious orders, and more kinds of prayer than any single person could really come to know in a mortal lifetime. There are over a billion Catholics living on earth, speaking thousands of languages, each individual coming to a different experience of closeness to or distance from what he or she thinks of as God. Surely among all of that dizzying variety of ways to experience Catholicism, there is room for a more sustained conversation about what it might mean to be a Catholic agnostic, or a Catholic atheist, or a lapsed Catholic who still clings to Catholic identity, or a returned Catholic who comes bearing the gifts of knowing how to move through the secular world, who lives life in conversation and relationship primarily with people outside of the church. Rather than struggling to define who gets to be Catholic by checking off mass attendance or sacramental participation or ways in which a person does or does not agree with the Magisterium, might we instead look at what it means to be Catholic by choice, even if that choice is often clouded with doubt?

Catholicism is also rife with doubters. John of the Cross, that melancholy Spanish mystic, tells us across the centuries that "if he wishes to be sure of the road he treads on, he must close his eyes and walk in the obscurity."[7] But usually we are urged to "pray confidently," to have "confidence in God's faithful love," to "trust" in God, to "believe." But these incantations are not magic; they cannot move someone from the periphery into the glowing place where trust and confidence and belief come with ease. Still, Pope Francis has spoken clearly about the need for doubt:

> In this quest to seek and find God in all things there is still an area of uncertainty. There must be. If a person says that he met God with total certainty and is not touched by a margin of uncertainty, then this is not good. For me, this is an important key. If one has the answers to all the questions—that is the proof that God is not with him. It means that he is a false prophet using religion for himself. The great leaders of the people of God, like Moses, have always left room for doubt.[8]

I think the pope is stating something many of the Catholics I interviewed would agree with. The questions many bring with them

---

[7] John of the Cross, *The Complete Works of Saint John of the Cross*, trans. David Lewis, ed. Oblate Fathers of Saint Charles Book 2, *Of the Night of the Spirit*, chap. 16, "How the Soul Journeys Securely When in Darkness" (London: Longman, Green, Longman, Roberts, and Green, 1864), 1:425.

[8] Pope Francis, in Antonio Spadaro, SJ, "A Big Heart Open to God: The Exclusive Interview with Pope Francis," *America* (September 30, 2013).

will last a lifetime and will never be answered in a language that makes sense. One learns to negotiate them enough to stay in the church, learns to redirect them into a kind of one-foot-in-one-foot-out faith, or is just going . . . going . . . gone.

7

Boomerangs

"The Tattooed Feminist Catholic Who Chooses Conscience over Catechism." That was the somewhat sensationalistic headline the *National Catholic Reporter (NCR)* chose for a profile of a writer who'd been raised in the church, left it for a life of badly defined faux-atheism, and returned to the church, only to end up as a religion writer. That tattooed feminist was me. The *Reporter* is known for its willingness to push the envelope on difficult issues in the church; in 1968, it was officially condemned by the former bishop of Kansas City, Charles Helmsing, who wrote that the *Reporter* had a "disregard and denial of the most sacred values of our Catholic faith" and had "made itself a platform for airing heretical views on the church."[1] The current bishop of Kansas City, Robert Finn, recalled the condemnation in 2013 and demanded that the *Reporter* "submit its bona fides" as a Catholic media outlet.[2] The *Reporter* cited its status as an independent media outlet in its defense, but it continues to attract vitriol from some quarters of Catholicism, including blogger Father John Zuhlsdorf, who quaintly refers to the newspaper as "fishwrap."

But anyone who regularly reads the *Reporter* online may know it best for the people who populate its comment boards. Within a day or so of the profile being posted, it had accumulated nearly five

---

[1] "Text of *NCR* Condemnation: Bishop Helmsing Charges Heresy," *National Catholic Reporter,* October 16, 1968.

[2] Alex Smith, "Bishop Finn Condemns *National Catholic Reporter,*" February 4, 2013.

hundred comments. A friend who read them discovered that only one or two commenters seemed to have actually read the profile; the rest rapidly descended into finger pointing, name calling, and various *ad hominem* accusations, all of which amounted to the same thing: a bunch of people saying to one another, "You're not really Catholic." Progressive? "Not really Catholic." Moderate? "Not really Catholic." The only people who are really Catholic, in the world of the *NCR* comment boards and across much of the Catholic Internet, are the ones who are fully in agreement with every page of the *Catechism of the Catholic Church*.

So who gets to decide what it means to be "really Catholic"? When I put this question to several priests, I got back a complex and sometimes contradictory series of answers. One replied that anyone who was baptized counted as a member of the church. A friend currently studying canon law pointed me to Canon Law 204.1, which states that you not only have to be baptized, but also "share the profession of faith, the sacraments, and ecclesiastical governance" to be "considered in communion with the Church." Canon Laws 208–23 have much more specific rules for acting out the obligation of the laity, but some of those rules are ambiguously stated and hard to understand, including 209.1, which tells us that "the Christian faithful, even in their own manner of acting, are always obliged to maintain communion with the church," or 210, which says that Christians should try to lead a "holy life" but "according to their own condition." The linguistic ambiguity about what "their own manner of acting" or "their own condition" might be, however, has led to painful arguments and debates about what a person should do or be in order to be a part of the church.

What is clear, however, is that it is not easy formally to renounce your membership in Catholicism. Another priest told me he'd heard of people having ceremonies where they burned their baptismal certificates, but this is merely a gesture, not an official departure. The Archdiocese of Dublin issued this statement on October 12, 2010: "The Holy See confirmed at the end of August that it was introducing changes to canon law and as a result it will no longer be possible to formally defect from the Catholic

Church."[3] In short, once you become Catholic, you will always be Catholic. But there is little to no agreement about what being Catholic means.

With that kind of deep-seated ambiguity about the role of the laity in Catholicism, it's no wonder that so many Catholics are confused about whether they're really considered Catholic or not. In the wake of the very public bickering at the 2014 Synod on the Family about whether LGBTQ persons should be "welcomed" or "provided for," many queer Catholics felt alienated and confused. Were they still Catholic if they weren't welcomed? More bickering arose at the synod on the question of divorced and remarried Catholics, who are not allowed to take communion unless they receive an annulment. Are divorced and remarried Catholics still Catholic if they are prohibited from taking communion? Are you still Catholic if you only go to mass once a year, skip confession for decades, don't tithe to a parish, disagree with your pastor, use birth control, or have sex with someone whose genitalia are the same shape as yours?

The debate about who gets to be "really Catholic" extends to people who leave the church, often for valid personal reasons. A woman who's divorced and remarried outside the church and thus barred from receiving communion, for example, might find that the Anglican Communion will not bar her from the table. A queer man who is told not to act on his desire might decide that the label of "intrinsically disordered" is one he no longer wants to carry. Or, perhaps, like 71 percent of former Catholics interviewed by PEW in 2009, they "just drifted away" from the faith of their childhood.[4]

But a tiny percentage of Catholics who drift away eventually find themselves drawn back. They become "reverts": people who return to the pews. It's difficult to put a precise number on reverts, however, because the term assumes that once they return to the church, they'll stay. One statistical estimate from 2012 puts the number of people from all religions who have reverted at about

---

[3] Archdiocese of Dublin, "12/10/10 Statement on Formal Defections."

[4] Pew Research Center, "Interactive: Reasons for Joining, Reasons for Leaving," April 27, 2009.

9 percent.[5] CARA's 2008 projection puts it slightly higher, at 13 percent.[6]

Given the fact that roughly 13 percent of all Americans are former Catholics,[7] the odds that they will begin to return to the religion in droves are highly unlikely. For reverts, the decision to return means facing the not "really Catholic" question all over again. Oftentimes, what drove them from the church is exactly what they wrestle with when they return. And the experience of returning to the church and trying to find community and support can be lonely and isolating. Friends who also drifted from the church may view a revert's decision to return with suspicion; Catholics who never left can be critical of those who did and can sometimes accuse them of having a shallow sense of faith.

So what makes a person want to return to a church when she or he has seen it at its worst? Millennials and Gen X Catholics grew up in an era when the sex-abuse scandal was out in the open. We saw the outcomes of what generations of Catholics had endured at the hands of pedophiles and sadists. We knew that the two popes who proceeded Francis were strict on dogma and unfriendly to the social changes that had swept through secular society, that the structure of the church was irrelevant to much of the way that we lived. But our gut instinct, for better or worse, was that the baptism we received as infants wasn't going away. Something made us ask questions, turn back, reopen the door. Once we walked in, we had things to grapple with. Were we Catholic Nones? Were we staying or going? Did anyone care that we were back?

Of her Catholic upbringing, Joan says, "I wasn't totally sold on it." Twenty-seven years old and recently embarked on a career as a

---

[5] Cathy Lynn Grossman, "'Reverts' Return to Their Childhood Religions," *USA Today,* April 5, 2012.

[6] "America's Changing Religious Landscape: Christians Decline Sharply as Share of Population; Unaffiliated and Other Faiths Continue to Grow," PEW Research Center, May 12, 2015, http://www.pewforum.org.

[7] Ibid.

teacher, Joan, like many Catholics in her generation, drifted away from religion after an ambiguous introduction to it in her childhood. Her experience of faith was one of "[feeling] religious to the extent that I went to mass and had to practice the sacraments, and there was a guy I was supposed to love." She describes this version of religion as "normal for twelve-year-olds." Joan attended public school and went to weekly mass with her parents, whom she describes as "devout and private about their beliefs. It wasn't the topic of conversation at the dinner table. It wasn't enforced and they didn't push me to go to mass." In retrospect she realizes that "if they had pushed, it would have been the fatal push away."

In high school Joan was surrounded by "a lot of people who were not practicing Catholics, or they belonged to another denomination. So I wasn't around people who'd consider faith something everyday." The lack of religious exposure "probably made a difference" to the increased apathy about Catholicism Joan was beginning to feel as a teenager. She doesn't pinpoint anything specific that began to creep in, but more of a general lack of motivation to attend mass. And, perhaps, her parents' choice to let her make her own decisions about attending, she says, allowed her the freedom to choose not to go. Of her attitude toward religion at that time, she says she was "not against it. I just didn't care."

College was the beginning of her real exodus from identifying as Catholic. "It was a slow burn. I tried to go [to mass] my freshman year and think actively about praying. I had a rosary, and I'd say it once every couple of months, then that fell away." She admits that being in college made her want to "push back a little" against religion, particularly the campus nondenominational Christian groups that were "too pious for my liking" and whose politics clashed with her own increasingly progressive ones. Another issue that had begun to arise in high school was exacerbated by the stressful environment at college. Of her mental health, Joan says, "I did have some issues with anxiety that helped push that apathy [about religion] toward thinking about anything but myself." Anxiety, as it later turned out, would tie closely into Joan's relationship with religion.

"In high school and college I had panic attacks and didn't know what they were. I was twelve the first time I thought I was having a heart attack and said a rosary and started bargaining with God." God didn't take away the panic attacks, which worsened over time. Joan's coping mechanism, like many people with anxiety disorders, was to turn inward. It was "just me being really into myself. Not narcissistic but solipsistic. I was really only thinking about myself and my anxiety." The feedback loop of anxiety was a mystery to Joan's parents, who repeated the advice "to try praying, and my response was always no. It was never going to work." Medication didn't work well for Joan, and "prayer and mindfulness don't produce instant results. That's where that schism" between her anxiety and religion "got bigger and bigger, because the relief wasn't instantaneous." She describes the outcome as "going on my merry way, still anxious, but no further from or closer to faith."

College was also the beginning of Joan's exposure to some of the writers who would push her ideas about faith in unexpected directions. She read Flannery O'Connor for the first time, but without much knowledge of O'Connor's Catholic background. "If I had known she was writing from belief it would have made a difference, but I didn't know," she admits. She also encountered James Joyce, who was "reacting against and from Catholicism." But most of the writers she was encountering were "anti-anything that would pull me toward a faith system or spirituality based on something divine." French philosopher Michel Foucault exemplified the "super downer people" Joan encountered in literature classes. "No one should be that into Foucault," she sighs. While she was encountering "a lot of angry male writers," feminist writers also played their part in her questions about the role of religion. Feminist scholar "bell hooks was making me question everything about my beliefs and my position as a person of privilege." For Joan, these writers "were inducing a lot of guilt, and I didn't think anyone could do that better than Catholics." She describes the English department at her college as "very radical and against anything religiously leaning." The more time she spent reading work that questioned the purpose of religion in society, the more she felt an apathy toward the Catholicism of her childhood. Of this education in secularism, she says, "I was into that. I was very much interested" in a different way of seeing the world.

A few years later Joan was able to put this embrace of anti-religious thinking into perspective. "I just turned twenty-seven, and there's a huge difference from me at twenty-three. I . . . was parroting other people's ideas because I liked and respected them. But it wasn't what I truly believed. I'd pick up on people who I thought were cool and from different backgrounds." Nonetheless, even if religious feelings were still stirring underneath the glaze of postmodernism, deconstruction, and feminist theory, Joan was also beginning to understand that institutional Catholicism didn't always meet people where they had arrived. "I was seeing in a lot of ways that a lot of these people who were somehow 'othered' weren't welcomed in the church I was brought up in." As she headed off to do graduate study in writing, it seemed as if Joan's move away from religion was calcifying into a permanent departure.

But an unexpected change in career led Joan to a new way of thinking about religion. "I defended my thesis in August of last year." Up to that point, she'd been worried about landing a job, and had interviewed at a school "where a teacher had quit and they'd interviewed a few people, and for some reason chose me." She moved back to her hometown, back into her parents' house, "got the job the week before, defended my thesis, and started teaching, and I've been teaching ever since." When we spoke, at the end of her first year as a teacher, Joan admitted that "teaching high school is so hard. I was ridiculously immature before this, and I've grown a lot. A lot has to do with the profession itself." But her new career also brought her back into contact with something she'd deliberately turned away from: Catholicism. Her transition into maturity, she says, is also based on "the fact that it's a Catholic school, and I've been able to find my identity as a Catholic person. It's strange."

Moving back in with her parents wasn't too much of an issue for Joan because "they were wonderful about it," but it also meant deciding whether or not to start attending mass with them again.

"The first week I was home they asked if I wanted to go to church. They go and sing in the choir. I thought, since I live at home I'll do you a solid and go to mass." Joan began to realize that for many Catholics "mass is a perk and a nice experience," and she discovered that she actually enjoyed being back in a pew in spite of her past apathy toward religion.

But, like many younger Catholics, Joan brought her more progressive politics back into religious life along with her maturing self. "When I first started teaching at the school," she recalls, "I told everyone I'd be working at a Catholic school, and my grad friends said you can infiltrate them and tell them about birth control and gay marriage, and I was all for it." But as she got to know her teaching colleagues, she discovered that a direct confrontation with authority might not be the best route to the political infiltration her friends had imagined. She describes keeping quiet and avoiding talk "about anything other than teaching," and as the year went on, she began to realize that while "my politics didn't match up" with her more conservative and pious colleagues, "these people love these kids so much. It's a good environment."

Like many Catholic schools, the one where Joan teaches is thin on clergy and struggling financially. "The school hasn't been updated since the sixties. They just got an elevator. It just became a place where people who are differently abled could navigate." The demographics of her students are all over the map. "We are sort of this weird little animal. It's a small school and not in the best area. We have students from great privilege and great poverty." Those students, as it turned out, would be the key to her finding a way back into something that looks loosely like a Catholic identity.

Joan's school doesn't have a chapel on campus, so when it came time for the first school mass, they "set up chairs in the auditorium. A priest said mass and the students were really, really, really involved. They sang songs and did hand motions. I didn't know the songs, and I sat with my freshmen who didn't know the songs either, and the older students were trying to help them learn." For Joan, that moment of seeing her students at mass "wasn't a spiritual awakening, but it was nice to see kids genuinely like the experience. And then over the course of the year," she adds, pausing. "It wasn't an epiphanic thing," she finally continues. "I was growing toward something. The wonderful thing is how much emphasis the school puts on volunteering and service. They really make sure the kids are aware of how that's necessary not only to be a good Catholic, but a good human being, and the kids respond positively."

"Hearing teenagers talk so earnestly about their belief" spilled over into teaching English. Her students were able to tap into the deeply spiritual roots of much Western literature that many of her college and grad school professors had actively fought back against. Of her students, she comments, "They'd read poetry and see it as a spiritual thing. They saw every poem as a gift from God. Because they saw it that way, I was able to see it that way." Joan's students were open to interpretation of literature and saw that it "could have both God and nature or God and a human struggle. That was a metaphor for the school. You could have both religion and evolution, and those things could exist together. So that helped me see how those things could exist together."

Although she began to grow in her spiritual life and understanding of a more universal Catholicism through her work with students, Joan admits that "there are people at the school who have interpretations of Catholicism that make it hard to be a feminist. The faculty are wonderful," she says, but "some are a little . . . not open." Nonetheless, when it comes to negotiating this issue with her students, she chooses to see it as a pedagogical puzzle rather than an impenetrable divide. "Helping students negotiate these things has been kind of a fun challenge," she says of feminist issues. "Using the word of God and the words of humans together." And that has bled over into her own reconsideration of what it means to be Catholic. "Because I did it in class, I had to do it on my own time. That's been the linchpin. It's been a really satisfying experience to think about these things in conversation. I did a lot of reading and came across some opinions about existing between those two spheres" of secular and progressive politics and Catholic thinking. "Finding out there are middle-ground Venn-diagram things going on," she says, "makes it easier to be comfortable being a Catholic school teacher and being Catholic."

When I ask what keeps her going in a church that seems to contradict so much of how she defines herself as a feminist and free thinker, Joan replies that being back has helped her to see that, contrary to some lines of thinking, there is no single way to be Catholic. "I want to be a part of ensuring that the church as it pertains to the people is many voiced. I'd like my voice to be part of that. I'm not atypical in being someone with opinions that might be heretical or not to the 'big C church' opinion, but I'd like to be a part of the group of people that try to make the church something that is love."

And in her year of transformation into a teacher, Joan now understands that her young Catholic students are part of that potential for transformation as well. Of the potential for the church to be a place of acceptance and love, she says, "I want to help my students see that. I'm making it a goal to merge my politics and beliefs. I feel strongly about this because it's a conviction based on a love of humanity. That's related to what I was taught growing up. I want to make sure I'm a credible voice to my students, so I have to think intellectually and spiritually about things that are seemingly contradictory." Will the contradiction ever be solved for Joan? She doesn't know. But she does know one thing that keeps drawing her deeper into a life of faith. "One thing I really appreciate about Catholicism," she says, "is the idea of mystery."

For a little over a year Anne has been tracking her journey back toward Catholicism on her blog. In her posts she talks about wrestling with the church's stance on birth control and trying to find an open-minded parish in her very conservative home state; she also details her experiences in a marriage-prep course. Anne describes herself as a former atheist/agnostic who dabbled in Buddhism, which was beginning to be a track followed by many of the other people I'd interviewed. She came from an interesting juxtaposition of positions regarding religion, and I wanted to know whether her recent tentative steps back toward Catholicism had been troubled with any particular obstacles.

"I was raised Catholic," Anne says. Her mom came from a family of eleven kids; Anne attended Catholic school from kindergarten through third grade, surrounded by Catholic "best friends," doing "all the regular Catholic school things." After third grade her family moved, and she began attending public school. Anne was enrolled in CCD (catechism classes for children not attending Catholic school), but within a few years, her interest in religion began to fray. "I had my confirmation, and after that things kind of fell apart. I was in middle school, and I started questioning the beliefs a little bit, and I didn't get many good answers. At the time I noticed my priest wasn't being very inclusive. He'd talk about the beauty of other religions and say they were all wrong." Like many former Catholics, Anne found holes in the doctrine. When she poked at them, they only got wider and deeper. In particular, the church stance on birth control stood out as problematic. "I got older and learned about the stance on birth control. . . . Considering my grandparents had so many kids, it seemed old fashioned to hold that view." Her mother added to the growing distance between Anne and the church. "My mom was a single parent, and she tried to take me to church, but around that time she stopped taking me as much. She was also very angry at the church because she'd been divorced and felt she wasn't included."

The fraying connection finally broke in high school. By then, Anne "didn't consider myself Catholic any more. I applied to a Catholic college but checked that I wasn't religiously affiliated." In her college years Anne describes herself as "bouncing between atheist and agnostic." She was required to take religious studies classes but ducked out of anything related to Christianity in favor of classes titled "Eastern Religions" and "Religion and Personal Experience." "I wanted to stay really far away from theology, because I thought it wasn't relevant to my life." Anne had long had an interest in Buddhism and took the opportunity in college to "dabble" in it. "I felt like it was easier to believe in than Catholicism. There's a lot of room for different interpretations, and not everything was black and white all the time." For a person who was in the midst of seeking out a less strident form of religion, Buddhism, at that juncture, represented a kind of middle way: faith, but without the doctrine.

In these liminal years of college Anne was surrounded by Catholicism, but she found it easy to ignore. "My college had a lot of non-Catholic students." Of the students who were Catholics, they didn't often assert much of a Catholic identity. Her college did try to emphasize Catholic social teaching, but it didn't make a big impact on Anne at that point in her life. "The biggest thing my school did was try to instill Catholic values in us, but more like volunteering," she adds. "You'd see nuns walking around and stuff like that. But you didn't have to be involved in being religious if you didn't want to be." Her social life consisted of "friends who were Catholic and friends who weren't," and she began dating a guy who was "super Baptist and not very liberal."

She also considered making the same leap many frustrated liberal Catholics have and becoming an Episcopalian. "From the outside they seem to have many of the same beliefs and traditions as Catholics, and they tend to be more liberal." But when she began digging into church history, she discovered that the Episcopal Church had its roots in the political maneuvers around the divorce of Henry VIII and the beginnings of the Anglican Communion. "Maybe it's shallow of me," Anne says, "but I really preferred the rich history of the Catholic Church to the more dubious beginnings of the Anglican Church—not that Catholic history isn't full of problems, but it doesn't seem to have started out that way." She also struggled with the Protestant idea that faith alone could save a person. Anne felt that good works were just as important. "Maybe my preference for works is due to the fact that faith does not come easy to me," she admits. "When I went to confession and told the priest that I had considered myself an atheist, his advice was that no one is born with faith. It's something that we have to ask for." Years after her struggle to figure out where her faith life was going, she still finds it difficult to believe. "So lately I've been praying for faith, which feels super ironic."

The conservative Baptist boyfriend she met in college soon after became Anne's fiance, and as it turned out, it was he who opened the door to her looking back into Catholicism. "Last year in November I got engaged, so I'm getting married this year. Around that same time my fiance and I attended an engagement party for friends. And we happened to go to a Catholic church with them." Reentering the church, even for the length of a mass, had a ripple effect on Anne's confusion about what her religious identity might be. Of that moment of being back in church, "I felt like I missed it. It reminded me of my childhood and brought me peace and comfort and that sort of thing." She returned home and started to think about the possibility of having kids in the future, and what it would mean to raise them without the structures of organized religion that had been part of her own life.

Still internally resistant to jumping back into Catholicism, Anne "was thinking of different religions to follow, but there's not much in my area. I thought about Unitarians and Buddhists, but they're both far away." At that juncture Anne read a quotation from the Dalai Lama, who, she paraphrases, said that it was better not to convert to Buddhism but to stay in your own religious tradition and bring Buddhist practice into it. "That led me a book called *Without Buddha I Could Not Be a Christian*" by Paul Knitter, who taught courses in religious pluralism at Union Theological Seminary. Of Knitter's book Anne says, "I don't think a Catholic priest would endorse it, but it really helped me to an understanding of God and Jesus and the stuff it was hard to believe in high school. So that made me think about the Catholic Church in another way." Anne's walk from agnosticism and back into Catholicism was beginning, in increments. Knitter's book "specifically talks about how it's okay not to get caught up in literalism, like virgin birth and the ascension." For Anne, this stance came as a relief. "It made me start to look at God in a different way. It talked about God as the interconnectedness between people. Love and peace, that's easier to believe in than just some deity. I don't know if the church would agree," she adds, "but it made it easier for me to understand it."

After college Anne moved to a large East Coast city. This became a pivot point in her relationship with church teachings on birth control and abortion. "I started working at an organization that works with nonprofit groups to fundraise. Some of those were pro-choice groups. So it was mostly street and door to door fundraising." Anne put her heart and conscience into the work. "I believed in it a lot and learned a lot about the issues." At that time there were "attacks on women's rights and attacks on access to birth control, personhood amendments that were trying to be passed. The birth-control part of the Affordable Care Act went into place at that point, which was very important." Anne's nonprofit would "always research the issues" before taking a stance on them, and in the process she began to identify the depths of the schism between the way most women live and the Catholic Church's understanding of that. "Every once in a while you'd see the Catholic bishops complaining and trying to stop the birth-control coverage. I felt like the Catholics and what I was doing didn't go together very well." She'd also read a feminist book in college about natural birth control as a means of empowerment, because women who used it weren't suppressing their fertility or giving money to male-dominated pharmaceutical companies. So, she says, she's "okay" with using fertility awareness herself, "but I don't want to tell other people what they should do. I wish the Catholic Church would reevaluate that."

Thoughts about family have increasingly colored Anne's life since she got engaged. Her boyfriend grew up Baptist but had a Catholic mother, and when she began debating attending church again, Catholicism "interested him more and more over the years. So we came to the decision together." Her fiance began the process of conversion. "We're going to have a religious wedding." They plan to marry at the church on the campus of the Catholic college where they met. "There's a lot of steps involved," she says with a laugh.

Since Anne and her fiance were already living together, in the culturally conservative part of the country where they now live, planning a Catholic wedding means encountering some potential obstacles. "It's really up to the parish and what they want to do" whether or not they'll question the couple's living situation. "There is another parish we looked at originally, but we went on Facebook and it said all kinds of stuff about liberals and it was ridiculous. So I felt they wouldn't be welcoming." But when Anne went to confession at another church and talked to the pastor about the work she'd done fundraising for birth-control awareness, "he didn't seem outraged or anything." Contradictions abound in Catholicism, but, as Anne discovered, they abound in Catholics too.

Of her steps to returning Anne admits that "it can be a little bit awkward being back. It was stressful the first few months. The time we got engaged was the time I thought about returning to church. I felt stressed about having a Catholic wedding and was probably putting more pressure on myself than I needed to." Her forays into learning more about the current state of the faith by searching through blogs and news sources on the Internet and in books made things more confusing and contradictory. "I'd be pro-Catholicism and then say I disagree with them. When you go online you find different books about people who became Catholic, and most of them embrace every aspect of Catholicism. I couldn't do that on some issues." Many books about Catholicism contributed to the problem of feeling like the cacophony of voices spoke only for the most extreme experiences of conversion. "It was hard to find voices similar to mine. A lot of books I found were about things like atheists who converted overnight and changed everything."

Mostly, she struggled to understand that "making abortion illegal will solve anything." She's not against the idea of following church teaching, and she wants to have children eventually, but she also sees the problem through the lens of someone who spent time advocating for women's ability to make their own decisions about the process. Like the 72 percent of religious Americans who believe it is acceptable to disagree with their faith on the issue of abortion and still remain a person of good standing within that faith, Anne's uneasiness about the Catholic Church's black-and-white approach to abortion issues is also increasingly common among Millennials, who support legal abortion by a fairly strong margin of 60 percent, even while they sometimes question its morality. For now, she says, "I've kept an open mind, and I've been listening to arguments about traditional church teaching," but admits that "a lot of them haven't stuck. I can live with the rules the best I can, but I can't see that they're best for everybody."

Being back, even with those questions still ringing in her mind, Anne finds herself at peace with occupying what might from the outside seem like a marginal space in the church. "So far the parish hasn't said anything that made me want to leave. I expect them to ask me to pray for the end of abortion, even if I don't always agree." Being out of sync with church teachings may mean that Anne is holding on to her gut instincts about women's rights, but "it does make me a little uncomfortable. If they knew what I was thinking, maybe they wouldn't want me there." Before she began attending mass again, that feeling of not being welcomed "was one of my biggest concerns." For now, however, she's discovered that maybe the message the church offers people like her is bigger than just the hot-button issues. "The priest hasn't really said anything in his homilies I disagree with. He's mostly focused on caring for each other. Nothing too controversial."

Perhaps what it means to be "really Catholic" means discovering the same things that Joan and Anne did, or that anyone who leaves the church and attempts to come back will discover. There is no one way to be "really Catholic," because a person's Catholicism is ultimately determined by how she or he chooses to live it out. Those of us who leave Catholicism are able to see it two ways: from within and without. If we return, we are both outsiders and insiders, able to see why people leave, but also able to understand what makes them stay. And reverts often see something that people outside Catholicism might miss. For all of the church's messaging about what people do with their bodies, what it is really concerned with are their souls. And the soul of a revert is one that is always in the process of questioning, discovering, and negotiating.

8

Sex, Marriage,
and the Unholy Mess

The Catholic parish closest to UC Berkeley's campus holds weekly dinners for Catholic students. Occasionally, they invite faculty from the university to join in at the dinner to talk with students and create some inter-generational dialogue about being Catholic at a deeply secular school. One evening I was among the faculty invited. Perhaps more so than any other public university in America, Berkeley wears its secular culture as a badge of pride. The fiftieth anniversary of the Free Speech Movement, which had occurred just weeks before the student dinner, was occasion for widespread celebrations and rallies, and free copies of a biography of Mario Savio were given out to all freshmen.

Meanwhile, when a student of mine asked if Berkeley had a religious studies major, Berkeley's sheer size (forty thousand students, more than two thousand faculty members), and a large number of academic programs (350) meant that I couldn't answer the question without Googling it. It turned out that the Religious Studies program was an interdisciplinary major that "views religion from a global perspective and combines aspects of the humanities and the social sciences." This seemed promising to me and my student, both interested in the intersections of religion and culture, but when we clicked over to a list of faculty, we landed on a blank page. When we clicked again to a list of courses, we hit another blank page. Perhaps it was just a coincidence and typical of Berkeley's erratic updating of department websites, but at that moment it spoke volumes about the confusing life people who are interested in religion can encounter at Berkeley. On Sproul Plaza students may encounter dozens of evangelicals actively trying to recruit them, but there is little dialogue between people of faith and nonbelievers, unless it involves shouting or running away from an out-thrust flyer.

The students I sat with at the faculty dinner were unfailingly polite, although it was awkward for all of us to be socializing outside of a classroom or office hours, and of the Catholic faculty who attended, I was one of two who were not retired. The generation gap yawned on either side. We chatted about classes and majors and the cultural differences between STEM and humanities; we talked about midterms; and eventually, we got around to religion. As it turned out, I was seated across from a religiously devout graduate student who led a Bible study in his apartment and was curious as to why the parish didn't offer a Latin mass. On my other side a young woman who ran the mailing list for the church's meals for the homeless program talked with me about how much social justice mattered to her and how she struggled to stay engaged in working with the homeless on top of school and work. But when we got around to the subject of marriage and dating, she was adamant; "I would never date someone who wasn't Catholic," she said with finality. The Latin mass guy was a little more realistic, saying that it was pretty likely, given their demographic, that she might well wind up dating a non-Catholic, but she insisted it was not going to happen. "We'd be too different," she replied, with a shake of her head.

Weeks later I sat in a circle at RCIA, where for several years I'd been assisting the team that runs the weekly meetings for people interested in Catholicism. Many people participating in RCIA were there because they were dating or engaged to Catholics. We had invited several people from the parish to come and talk about their own experiences of Catholicism, and among the guests were a couple who'd been married for eighteen years before the husband, raised in an atheist family, had converted.

In answer to a question about marriage from one of the people dating a Catholic, the wife insisted that "our marriage is so much better now. I thought I could never date a non-Catholic, and it was such a relief when he finally saw it wasn't just doctrine and dogma." An older gentleman added that his own wife wasn't Catholic and that "she misses out on so much" as a result and that he "felt badly" for her that she didn't want to convert. I looked over at my fellow team member, who is married to a Jewish guy, and gave her an empathetic look before replying, "Some of us can be happily married to non-Catholics." For millennia, the church had insisted that marriage was best if both parties were Catholic. So why were so many Catholics marrying non-Catholics? Why were some Catholics so adamant about finding someone of the same faith? As with every other question about the role of religion in what increasingly looked like a post-religious society, the answer was muddled and convoluted at best.

In the past few decades the Catholic definition of marriage, and traditional notions of what marriage means to Catholic lives, has been challenged in ways it did not expect. The rapid proliferation of legalized same-sex marriage in the United States (thirty-seven states recognize same-sex marriage as of this writing) led to the US Conference of Catholic Bishops organizing a "March for Marriage" in Washington DC in June 2014, hoping to rally faithful Catholics who support the notion that marriage can only exist between a man and a woman. Only about two thousand people showed up to the bishops' event,[1] in contrast to the attendance at San Francisco Pride, which was estimated at 1.2 million people.[2] In another area of human sexuality the Catholic Church has long insisted that married couples refrain from using birth control and instead rely on fertility awareness; however, the reduced number of children born into Catholic families makes it obvious that most Catholics are not following the *Catechism* in that regard.[3]

---

[1] Paul Best, "March on Marriage Fails to Attract a Crowd at the Capitol, Gallup Knows Why," June 24, 2014, http://www.reason.com.

[2] Sam Whiting, Kale Williams, and Justin Berton, "Huge Crowd, Ecstatic Vibe at SF Gay Pride Parade," June 27, 2014, http://www.sfgate.com.

[3] "Supplemental Tables on Religion and Contraceptive Use," Guttmacher Institute, unpublished tabulations of the 2006–8 National Survey of Family Growth.

As to the odds that a young Catholic person would wind up marrying another Catholic, they too are increasingly long: today, up to 40 percent of marriages are interfaith.[4] With the increasing number of nonbelievers in Gen X and Gen Y, many Catholics face greater odds that they may well end up dating or deciding to marry one of them. The church refers to Catholic marriages to those who haven't been baptized as a "disparity of cult," probably a bad translation of the Latin *disparitas cultus,* but not an encouraging turn of phrase. The *Catechism* advises that these marriages "risk experiencing the tragedy of Christian disunity even in the heart of their own home"[5] and requires that these couples receive a special dispensation if their wedding is to take place in a church. In light of my question about these shifts, the couple who runs the marriage-prep workshop for Catholics at my parish told me that every year, fewer and fewer people enroll.

Is this a sign that Catholic notions of marriage are fading away, that these young couples who insist that they would "never" marry a non-Catholic are outliers? Perhaps. Or, more likely, it may be a sign that marriage itself and our social concepts of family are evolving beyond something the institutional church is able to understand. In a PEW survey, only 30 percent of couples said that having a religious marriage ceremony was "very important." And the share of Americans who marry is shrinking every year: compared to 1960, when 72 percent of Americans were married, today, only 50.5 percent are.[6] Divorce still breaks up about half of all marriages, and more and more couples are choosing to live together and not get married at all. Same-sex marriage and people living in nontraditional family arrangements are all on the rise. The kind of marriage my parents had in the 1960s—same faith, same race, same culture, lots of kids, no divorce—is, by today's standards, somewhat unusual.

---

[4] Stephanie Hanes, "Interfaith America: 'Being Both' Is a Rising Trend in the US," *The Christian Science Monitor,* November 23, 2014.

[5] "Mixed Marriages and Disparity of Cult," in *Catechism of the Catholic Church,* 2nd ed. (Vatican: Libreria Editrice Vaticana, 2012), 455.

[6] Drew Desilver, "5 Facts about Love and Marriage," Pew Research Center, February 14, 2014.

Beyond marriage, too, there is the question of how religion might matter in friendships, community, and constructing a "chosen family." In the past it was easy for young people to find tribes of other Catholics to befriend; my parents, for example, were friends with several other large Catholic families, thrusting the kids into hanging out whether we liked one another or not. But we were all Catholic. So was most of the neighborhood. That would be an anomaly in many urban areas today. In fact, many young Catholics I spoke to said they'd rather keep their Catholicism hidden in social settings to avoid being grilled about controversial topics. Even if they insisted they'd rather date another Catholic, they still primarily socialized with religiously mixed groups.

Yet some young people continue to parse the demanding notions of what constitutes a traditional Catholic marriage. They refrain from premarital sex, don't live together before the wedding, and attend church-sponsored pre-Cana workshops, some of which involve going out of town for multiple weekends—not an easy task for working adults. They sit through meetings with priests, file paperwork with the diocese. But occasionally, these people are unprepared for what comes next. And sometimes, marriage pushes them further from God.

Emily responded to a query I'd posted on Twitter about marriage and the increasing number of ex-Catholics in the Millennial generation with a succinct message: "I've got a story for you." We met on a windy and bright April afternoon at a cafe on the Embarcadero in San Francisco and sat at an outdoor picnic table while cyclists and skateboarders skidded along the edge of the bay. The wind blew Emily's long auburn hair around while she spoke, thoughtfully and at length, about how the church's notions of marriage had turned her faith inside out. Emily had recently moved to San Francisco from Michigan, where, "I was raised Catholic and went to very traditional Catholic schools." Her family had "no money," but they managed to send all of their children to Catholic school, the same school where Emily's mother had gone and that her grandfather had helped build. Her Catholic roots were deep and enmeshed. "Dad was even Jesus in the Passion Play. I put the blood on his back."

Throughout Emily's childhood, parish politics "informed my Catholic experience." At one point those parish politics "became so intense that we started shopping around for another church. It was challenging for my parents," who had invested their time in the parish for decades. After sixth grade Emily was so put off by the bickering and arguing she witnessed within the parish that "I didn't want to go" to Catholic school any more. Her father got yelled at for making suggestions about improving the parish, and "he was visible and vulnerable" in his role as a leader there. Emily attended a "religiously mixed" public school briefly, but her mom stongly objected to the effect that was having on Emily's ideas about faith, and her father immediately sent her back to Catholic school. Eventually, she went to a public college, Michigan State, "intentionally."

But before that she stuck it out long enough in Catholic school to make it to confirmation, which she describes as "the most important thing, and really intense." Confirmation, in spite of the tumultuous background of parish life, began to push Emily into questioning the idea of what her vocation might be. "I started to think about being a nun. I broke up with a guy many times over this. It went on through college, the sense of calling and purpose." But beneath that calling, tectonic shifts were taking place within the foundations of her faith. She wondered how to be in religious life "without a religious structure. I tend to harp on God. I want to know what my purpose is." In college she pursued an Alternate Spring Break, traveling to work at an orphanage in Mexico that was run by Catholic sisters. "I thought I'd get exposure, and see how it felt." The result was that "it felt meaningful," but it also led to an epiphany about vocation and what that would mean for her life. "We were doing manual labor one day, and the lead sister was playing a guitar. I stopped and said 'I know this isn't for me.' That was the moment I had peace about it."

Instead of coming home and leaving religion behind, Emily made a decision that still has repercussions for her life today. "I got married at twenty, and did the whole Catholic marriage prep and mass." She and her equally young husband had been trying to adhere to the church's expectations about premarital sex. "We were saving it for marriage." Without going into further details, Emily admits that "the saving it thing was not the best idea." Whatever happened, it was bad enough that the marriage "totally blew up in my face. So that was it. It was done." The dissolution of the marriage was bad enough that it had a ripple effect throughout Emily's family as well. Her parents, the same parents who had insisted on her attending Catholic school and had poured so much of their lives into the church, "also disconnected at that point." They stopped attending church, losing an anchor that had gone back for generations. "They wanted this for me, and discouraged us from living together and saw that went wrong. That rattled them."

In the wake of her broken marriage Emily went looking for answers about what it would mean to leave the church behind, and she found the ones that finally pushed her out. "Sex abuse also made me vote with my feet, the role of women, picking on nuns who were my heroes." She listened to Dominican Sister Laurie Brink's 2007 speech to the Leadership Conference of Women Religious, which resonated with Emily even though it was an address to a group of women religious. In that speech Brink stated, "We have lost our prophetic place on the margins, having gravitated toward the middle of society and fallen off the edge of the church."[7] Emily says that Brink's speech and reading the work of the scholar Elaine Pagels, especially *The Gnostic Gospels,* helped her to understand that while she could no longer participate as a Catholic, she did not want to leave it entirely behind. Solidarity seemed to be a kind of middle way. "I don't see myself in the church but with people from the church."

"Not being in the institution feels more individualistic," Emily reflects. As to my question about the loss of a community, she replies, "I don't mind the solitude and sojourning. People have to accept the individual's seeking." She adds that for her father, the

---

[7] Laurie Brink, "A Marginal Life: Pursuing Holiness in the Twenty-first Century," Leadership Conference of Women Religious, August 2, 2007.

struggle in leaving the church (although he eventually returned) was different, because "he needs the community." For Emily, the version of faith she has now is less about the group and more about healing the wounded self. "I worry about being too intellectual and not spiritual. But spirituality doesn't only happen in a community." She admits that leaving Catholicism has caused a gap to open up in her life, one that looks a lot like nostalgia. "That's a good word for it. I love the saints and the mystic tradition and that's my community." At her grandfather's funeral singing the hymns and the ritual of the mass reminded her that "the ritual makes life more full and connected." But, "I can't co-opt that. I can't have my cake and eat it too."

Emily is remarried now to a man who was raised as a strict Baptist but who is "more of a scientist than a seeker. We both have a sense of wonder but explain it in different ways." She writes poetry, meditates, and tries to find space in conversations with friends to talk about the religious and the spiritual. "It's a mixed bag in my peer group." One religious friend just got engaged. She said it wasn't practical to wait for marriage. "As an adult," she adds, "you learn the exception." Her siblings are groping their own way through decisions about whether to stick it out in the church or not. "My younger brother is a fair-weather Catholic. My middle brother is the most traditional, but he asked both of us to be godparents." She laughs at the idea of being a godparent who isn't sure if she believes in God. "I don't want to co-opt that, but I like the subversion. He knows what I am, but he wants one traditional godparent and one less traditional one." But after the trauma and shakeup her marriage brought to the family, they do have one thing in common in their relationship to the church. "They all seem to waver." As we pack up our bags and walk back up the Embarcadero toward Market Street, she adds one last thing. "Catholicism," she reflects, "has a shadow side . . . and a lot of depth."

When I ask about his recent bout of spiritual seeking, Peter replies, "I'm still trying to figure out why I hit this up in such a way." A thirty-something father of two, he's sitting in front of his computer in a Midwestern state when we connect on Skype, and his wife and kids occasionally crisscross through the scene in the background. Peter had been leaving comments on some of my essays and tweets, and they seemed to indicate that while he'd been Catholic for a while, changes in his family and career were forcing a reconsideration of what role religion was going to play in his life. When I asked what kicked off the questions about religion that he was grappling with, he replied that he'd "read a book called *Forming Intentional Disciples*" by Sherry Weddell. It "spelled out the path of maturing in a spiritual life. There's a gap between liking having rules and following Christ. I want to form a relationship rather than just read books."

Unlike Emily, Peter never left the Catholic Church. But like many Catholics who stay in the church, he was struggling to understand how to live a religious life in a secular world, and his questions about believing and belonging were complicated by marriage and family. He had married another Catholic, but one who came from a different background and cultural notion of the role of religion. Having kids and going through several drastic career changes that led to multiple moves across states had uprooted his faith practice, and he was struggling to find a way to re-root it, while simultaneously realizing that for people in their thirties and forties, it is difficult to find any kind of community of peers in the church. Right now he finds a lot of his spiritual community online, through social media. After his kids were born, "life became more stable and job became less important. My career moved. I started to see the pointlessness of making a lot of money. Chasing after jobs didn't matter, and realizing that helped me focus on other things." That meant backing up and reconsidering the faith of his childhood.

In the midst of career and family shifts Peter "realized this part of me was important," but how to bring it into a more active role in his life wasn't clear. When he started looking around locally for other Catholics his age who wanted to talk about faith issues, perhaps start a Catholic Worker house or engage in some sort of faith-based social justice practice, he drew a blank. "I want to get all the families together because people don't want to talk about their faith. People didn't . . . . They weren't at that step. There aren't a lot of people my age doing that." He started attending a meeting of secular Franciscans, but "people were in their sixties and it's completely different" in terms of where they are in their experiences of religion. Attempts at ecumenical talk led to the conclusion that "conversations weren't necessarily deeper" with Protestants or nondenominational Christians. Of all this effort, he says, "I still don't know if it makes me better at faith—I'm just attuned to it more."

When I ask if this generational isolation bothers him, he says that he grew up in Florida "surrounded by elderly people," so that wasn't entirely the issue behind this unsettled feeling. "Church in general does a poor job with young and middle-aged people. Protestants do small groups and family things." In his experience, Catholics don't. Peter did encounter other parents in their thirties at mass, but "maybe they're just there because of kids." What he seemed to be grappling with, in some ways, was the same sensation inherent to many Nones: that the spiritual feeling of searching never seemed to come to any sort of conclusion. For Peter and other Catholics, even the tools the religion handed them—prayer, mass, dogma, liturgical seasons, rituals, and sacraments—did little to ease the sense that they were still searching for something deeper. Spiritual kinship, one of the ways to find that depth, proved difficult. His attempts to find community at church were fruitless. "Maybe it's because the other searchers aren't there. Maybe people don't go on spiritual searches in their thirties and forties. Maybe that's more of an end of life thing."

An intercultural marriage complicated this journey. "My wife is Peruvian and culturally Catholic." They met while he was traveling in Peru, and "she didn't get confirmed until we got married." When they met, his wife's South American Catholicism revealed some stark differences in their understandings of how to practice their faith. "It's interesting, because she didn't really know how to pray. She's not really sure what to do with tools of traditional prayer. All the external things and affectations, she just doesn't feel." For historical reasons, too, including the legacy of colonialism and missionary culture, Peter's wife never felt the same connections to ritual and structured prayer practice that he took for granted as an American. Of his wife's neutrality and conflict about Catholicism, he says, "If the religion was part of the subjugation of your people, that's part of not being concerned as much" about mass and prayer. To her, "it makes some of the American things we do kind of odd and silly."

Peter's kids are five and three years old, a little young to be grappling with questions and doubts, but he wants to give them room for both of those things. "It's important to model whatever spirituality you have. I think a life without that is empty." But he also understands that they're going to grow up in an increasingly secular and religiously diverse culture. In terms of religion, he says, "I'd teach them about anything—I'm a big defender of public education, but I'm sending them to Catholic school." When I ask why, he says that he wants to provide a grounding in knowledge about religion. But later on he will allow the kids to decide whether they will go to Catholic or public school. "Will I give them the choice? Yes." But for now, he says, "I want to give them something to go on."

This desire to expose his children to religious pluralism extends beyond the immediate family and into the extended household he's building along with his kids and his wife. For several years now they've hosted foreign-exchange students from nearby colleges. This year, one is a practicing Muslim. "I look forward to their getting to know other ways to be spiritual, and this is the way I can do it." Recently, he polled friends about ways to incorporate prayer into their family life. Another friend with kids suggested a short and simple ritual: "They each choose a prayer candle and say a prayer and blow out the candle. That's it." For Peter, introducing his kids to religion is about letting them decide what religion means. "You have to let them lead, see what they're responding to, and build on it," he says. If it sticks, great. If not, that's okay too. "I won't be heartbroken if they want to be a priest or bail on it. I just want them to know there's more to life." He also says that for him, religion helps to edge him away from America's consumer culture and obsession with wealth, and that's something he also hopes to pass along to his kids, whether they stay in a religion or not.

This desire to make family a kind of miniature church extends into Peter's planning for their future. "We almost went on a Mary-knoll mission," but at the time, "it didn't feel right." He has been skipping Sunday mass in favor of attending a daily mass when he can, because "Sunday mass is a place of frustration. When you go in the mornings it feels different," more intimate, more familial, and less like a consumer experience. But Peter still feels a sense that he's seeking something in his faith life that the institutional church isn't quite stepping in to fulfill. "I'm waiting to see if this is answering a call," he says of his spiritual restlessness. "I'd like to let things flow a little bit more, have less control, and be more accepting."

More recently, he's been looking back into the Third Order Franciscans, a lay group that takes a modified form of the same vows Franciscan friars and sisters take, but, he says, "I feel pressure about trying to find what I'm supposed to be." Is that an internal pressure or an external one? It's a little of both. Of being a seeker, "I'm in that boat now. Praying for years, and now what?" He watched recently as his sister left the Catholic Church, converted to Protestantism, and returned to Catholicism again. Wanting to avoid that boomerang move, Peter is trying to find alternate ways to build church in his life. When I ask what it means for him to be a Catholic parent, he says, "I'm trying to find meaning in being here and hoping."

Davey's relationship to Catholicism has also been marked by marriage and family issues, but in a radically different way from Peter's. Years ago Davey was a student at a Catholic college in a graduate class for which I was a teacher-assistant. Later we became friends and both worked as journalists, orbiting around the East Bay punk scene. After I began writing about religion, a conversation that started out being about writing revealed something I hadn't previously known about his family. His father had been a priest, and his mother had been a nun. When I asked if he'd be willing to talk about that at length, he agreed. Davey travels a lot—he's a full-time journalist in the auto industry and was about to leave to cover a car launch in Abu Dhabi. When he's not on the road, he lives in the central California city where he grew up rather than New York or LA, because his parents are facing health issues that have led to extensive conversations about mortality. So we talked at a time when Davey was already thinking about faith, family, and the complex web that connects him to Catholicism, even while he doesn't consider himself a practicing Catholic.

When I ask how his parents met, he says, "I don't really know the full story. Dad's always been weirdly private about it." He does know that his father went to UC Berkeley to be a premed student, but at some point "realized he only wanted to be a doctor for the money, so he did a 180 and became a priest." This was in the late 1950s and early 1960s, so the diocese sent his father to "a crazy deprogramming seminary, because he didn't go straight from high school." Eventually, his father wound up at a parish in Menlo Park, California, but was "always in poor neighborhoods" as a priest. Davey's mother grew up in Northern Ireland, "with limited options for women." When she turned eighteen, like many Irish women in her generation, she went straight into the convent. At some point her order "shipped her off to LA and put her through college." After college she taught, and when her order needed a sister to be the principal of one of its schools, she wound up in Sacramento.

By the time they met, "it was post–Vatican II, so there was a lot of liberalization," Davey says. His father "was more concerned with his community than politics in the diocese. It was a heavily black neighborhood, and he'd put a basketball team together. They won lot of games, and that raised some hackles because they weren't all Catholic." After that, his dad's "scientific training kicked in," and he realized that he was "being sold a bill of goods." At the same time his mother was "wrestling with things in the church I'm not entirely clear on." His parents left religious life in 1973; Davey was born two years later. His parents were in their late thirties by then, and he would turn out to be their only child.

"They exposed me to the church," Davey says, but it wasn't an in-depth exposure. "Most instructive" of his parents' approach to religious education "is my first communion." In 1985, his grandmother was coming to visit from Northern Ireland. A week before she arrived, Davey and a friend were hanging out, and when he asked his dad if he could stay at his friend's house, his dad said no because they were going to church in the morning, and, he says, "I thought that was weird," because they didn't attend very often. "Dad showed me how to make the sign of the cross and said I'd get a wafer." But that was it as far as catechesis about first communion was concerned. "I figured that was just something you did when you got to a certain age." Years later, on a visit to family in Ireland his cousins were showing pictures from their own first communions, and he realized that his parents had been "keeping up appearances for Grandma's sake."

When I ask what his parents' relationships are like to the church now, he says that his mom, "although she grew up more traditional and devout," is more willing to be critical. His father, however, is "hesitant to criticize it. He doesn't have much tolerance for people who are disrespectful of it." He does recall that at some point his father told him that when he and his mother were left religious life, they were trying to "seek the truth." "My dad is more sort of rigidly Catholic, and my mom is more cosmic and spiritual." It's a cultural reversal, he thinks, for a Californian father and an Irish mother. For Davey, his parents' mixed relationships with Catholicism left him in an in-between state, but he admits that he's inherited some of his father's reflexive defense of the religion. "Even though my relationship with Catholicism is tenuous, I have some of that weird 'yeah, okay, I disagree with this BS,' but it's an ingrained thing. Maybe it's an Irish thing. You don't want to get shot by the wrong people."

Davey attended public school all the way through high school, but when it came time to choose a college, "Catholic college was my choice." The school offered him good financial aid "because of my parents' previous careers," but "some of it was me wanting to connect with those roots." He'd never asked his parents much about their lives as a priest and nun, so he thought that going to a Catholic college would help him develop a deeper relationship with religion. "When I was seventeen, it made sense." Davey attended Saint Mary's College, a small liberal arts Catholic college in the East Bay suburbs run by the De La Salle Christian Brothers.

Davey, who had never spent extended time around people in religious orders, discovered at Saint Mary's that he "liked the brothers a whole lot. They were really seekers. That's what I enjoyed about them. They were more liberal than some of the lay faculty. Radical and interesting and challenging. I relished the classes I had with brothers." In the late 1990s Saint Mary's brought in a new president. From the beginning, Davey, along with other students, felt he was a bad fit for the school. The brothers Davey had come to know as teachers had been rigorously intellectual, challenging, and thoughtful. In contrast, the new president struck Davey as bad news. "The minute I met him," he says, "I thought, he's not a Christian Brother, he's a wannabe CEO." In 2004, the president resigned when a board member backed out of $112 million in pledges for building projects that had already begun. Two years later, after being hired at another college, he admitted to having had inappropriate sexual relations with a student at Saint Mary's and resigned once again.[8] The Saint Mary's community reeled, but the brothers who remained worked hard to rebuild trust among the students. "Otherwise," Davey says of his relationship to religion in college, "it all was generally positive. Definitely the more intelligent and less dogmatic side of Catholicism, for sure. I really enjoyed that."

Seeing the intellectual side of Catholicism helped Davey to come to some new understandings about the church. "The Catholic Church is so big and broad, but pieces are amazing and rad and full of history, and there's a tradition of rebels and challengers and thinkers." But like many younger Catholics, having been through scandals like the one at Saint Mary's, or having been alienated by the more rigid Catholicism of the two previous popes, Davey also sees why so many younger people distrust the church. "Until the

---

[8] Scott Jaschik, "Incident Catches up with a President," *Inside Higher Ed,* December 21, 2006.

[election of Pope Francis], so much that rolls downhill from the Vatican is like, 'really?'" He mentions the situation at my parish (the new bishop removed our priests) as an example of the kind of thing that keeps him at a distance. Of that, and of many other issues of clericalism and institutional failure, he says, "We're still doing this in the twenty-first century?"

After college, Davey "did punk rock stuff and drank a lot, and wasn't connected to anything spiritual in any meaningful way except via relationships. That was unhealthy, because you're putting faith in a fallible person. So I'd drift and drink more." He wound up in the suburbs of LA, where he started attending AA meetings, "which was a whole 'nother education in spirituality." Davey found that AA was a mixed bag: "There's a lot of dogmatic BS attached to that," he says, "but it's also kind of an anarchist group." The first meeting he attended in Southern California "was fantastic and diverse . . . the Jesus lady, longshoremen, gangsters figuring out how to live outside. People struggling with heavy stuff and doing it."

Davey moved on to do "a lot of meditation and long walks, and a lot of spiritual seeking of ethereal guidance kind of stuff." Once he'd achieved sobriety, he went gung-ho in search of a spiritual life, and "probably went a little cuckoo. Now that I wasn't numbing myself, stuff flooded in, and it took a couple of years to deal with that. Because my parents had tried to allow me to make my own decisions about religion and didn't give me any guidance, because they were afraid of me getting my head full of the stuff they got when they were young, I was kind of full of this energy I didn't know how to channel." Drinking, he says, had evened that out in the past. Sobriety meant confronting it.

After a time Davey "didn't go to church, but looped back toward Catholicism for a while, and sort of moved away again. I think my relationship to the church is a series of near misses. Like I orbit it. Obviously it's this powerful force in my life. I wouldn't be here without it. My origin story is completely rooted in it. And so I think that's probably the best way of putting it." But the gravitational pull of his family's immersion in Catholicism had never been a strong enough to keep him close enough to commit. His orbit around the church is "an eccentric orbit." Knowing Davey's proclivity for punk rock, fast cars, and other counter-cultural things, I ask if he thinks this core Catholic identity he keeps coming back to is, in its own way, counter-cultural. He recalls his father talking about the importance of Kennedy's election in the 1960s and says, "The dominant religious force in America is nebulous Protestantism. Catholicism seems much more vibrant. It's weird, but so is being a WASP. As much as I see the weird swaths of damage the church has caused when I look at America, it seems Catholicism is the least of its religious problems, or one of the lesser ones."

As he approaches forty, moves into a new job, and starts thinking about eventually starting a family of his own, he thinks of Catholicism as being "where I'm from. There's a claim to it and an ownership." His mother's family in Ireland brought this home throughout his childhood. "Especially when I was visiting family in Northern Ireland," he says, Catholicism is "the side you're on. I had guns pointed at me by the British Army, and it doesn't feel good." But, he adds, that's when his gut instinct to claim his parents' faith kicked in. "Sure I'm Catholic, because you're pointing a gun at me." Of that response, "It's kind of weird. I don't want to say it's reactionary. It's a lot of stuff." And he comes back to his family, again. Catholicism, for Davey, whether he participates or not, and whatever happens to his parents' relationships with the church as they approach the end of their lives, is "really just where I'm from. That is the closest thing."

The college kids at the dinner who said they would never date a non-Catholic have good intentions; they want a sacramental marriage, want faith to be at the center of their lives, want to be able to see their children baptized, and want to hand faith down to those kids. But marriage is nothing if not a complex set of negotiations that in some cases can go on for decades. In long marriages, and even in short ones, it's inevitable that some aspect of the involved parties' relationships with religion might shift. Emily, Peter, and

Davey all saw their relationships with Catholicism adjust through the experience of marriage, both their own and their parents'. And they are all members of generations that have seen marriage itself change and take on new meanings, ones that will continue to affect the kids born into a time when so many people are moving away from religion.

But marriage, religious or not, is ultimately about making a choice to merge one's life with someone else's and potentially to bring new life into the world as well. Anyone who has been married would probably agree that this is not always a seamless process, and questions of religion and belief can rough up the edges of those seams. Many years ago at a wedding I heard an officiant say that whatever role God was going to play in the proceedings, ultimately his own role was just formalism; the two people standing there were the ones choosing to marry each other. Religion may be like that officiant, providing a framework for people making a choice, a framework into which they may or may not be able to fit. And, in the case of Catholic marriage, while the framework may remain the same, the people within it will constantly be changing: in their love for each other in their concept of marriage, and in their notions about God.

9

Catholic Roots, Broken Branches

In a 2014 interview with the *Jesuit Post*, poet and critic Dana Gioia talked about the most influential living Catholic writers. After running off a checklist of some well-known names, his list wound up being relatively short, with only five writers who "have a plausible claim to posterity." He added a caveat: "If we move into the world of cultural Catholics, then there is a much larger group to choose from."[1] But what, exactly, is a "cultural Catholic"? It's a term that's long been tossed around to refer to everyone from, for example, Europeans whose family roots are Catholic but who rarely go to mass and don't bother adhering to many church teachings, to people who were baptized but never practiced the faith, to those Christmas and Easter Catholics, who show up at mass twice a year. They might also be called Two-Timers, Chreasters, C&E Catholics, Poinsettia, and Lily Catholics, CAPE Catholics (Christmas, Ash Wednesday, Palm Sunday, Easter), PACE Catholics (just mix up the letters), CASE Catholics (Christmas and Sometimes Easter), CMEs (Christmas, Mother's Day, and Easter) and A&P Catholics (Ashes and Palms).[2]

But this is all pejorative language poking fun at the fact that only 41 percent of American Catholics report that they attend weekly mass; Pew Research reveals that Catholics report attend-

---

[1] Jay Hooks, SJ, "Catholic Writing Today: Dana Gioia," *Jesuit Post,* January 23, 2014.

[2] "Lapsed Catholic: Colloquial Names," Wikipedia.

141

ing mass more than they actually bother to turn up.[3] Gioia uses the term "cultural Catholic" to talk about authors like Cormac McCarthy, Don DeLillo, and George R. R. Martin, all of whom were baptized and grew up Catholic, and all of whom are also old enough to remember Latin mass, Catholic immigrant enclaves in urban neighborhoods, and the pre–Vatican II church as a dominant, shaping force in their lives. DeLillo, when asked about the influence of the Italian immigrant Catholicism he grew up surrounded by in the Bronx, told a reporter that Catholicism "has an effect in ways I can't be specific about—the sense of ceremony, the sense of last things, and the sense of religion as almost at times an art."[4] For Gen X and Millennial Catholics, born after the sort of liturgies that seventy-eight-year-old DeLillo was steeped in had mostly vanished, those same traces of ceremony were only faintly felt.

Among the people who responded to my initial requests for interviews for this book, many identified as cultural Catholics, but each of them defined the term in a different way. There was little to no consensus about what being culturally Catholic meant. Some used it to describe ethnic roots in Latin or Central America, Mexico, Ireland, or Southern Europe. Some used it to talk about the oppressive force that had driven their parents away from religion one generation back. Boomers, after all, were the first generation to start moving away from the church in large numbers as ethnic Catholic culture broke up and mass going started to lose its sense of obligation. The cracking open of the sex scandals in the 1980s took more Boomers out of the church; seeing the damage done by priests, bishops, archbishops, cardinals, and popes of their own generation, men they'd known and trusted, their sense of betrayal made it impossible to keep going. In many cases they took their Gen X and Millennial children with them.

Culturally Catholic might not mean much any more in America. As the Catholic culture that formed a framework around the

---

[3] Denver Nicks, "No 'Francis Effect' for American Catholics," *Time Magazine,* November 25, 2013.

[4] Alexandra Alter, "What Don DeLillo's Books Tell Him," *Wall Street Journal,* January 30, 2010.

generation of writers Gioia refers to vanishes, the connections that Boomers had to Catholic immigrant roots from their own parents and grandparents grow more and more distant. In my parish it's not uncommon to hear Boomer parishioners say that their children and grandchildren are no longer part of the church. And for people whose own parents were burned by Catholicism or simply turned off by it, they may have a tiny, tenuous connection to the religion, but it looks more like Catholic roots than Catholic culture.

What younger people often talk about when they separate from a religious practice is the loss of, and the longing for, a sense of community. Each of us desires to be known. But for people whose own families struggled with religion and eventually distanced from it, those community ties feel tenuous. We are centuries past the agape meals of the early Christians. It's easy to romanticize the work of Dorothy Day and to forget the struggle that was a daily part of her life, but she tapped into this deep thirst for communion at the end of her memoir, *The Long Loneliness*: "We have all known the long loneliness," she wrote in 1952, "and we have learned that the only solution is love and that love comes with community."[5] Perhaps the falling away of Catholic culture, or even traditional notions of Christian culture, is more than just the loss of a particular age demographic or of rites, traditions and rituals. Culture, after all, means "to cultivate," and when a family leaves faith behind, what grows may not look like what went before. The roots become broken branches that somehow still grow, always seeking light.

Elizabeth grew up with Christianity and Catholicism hovering in the background rather than being at the forefront; her mother was Protestant, and her father "had a bad history with Catholicism specifically." In an interview we conducted over a series of emails, she writes, "No one in the family had religious convictions, but

---

[5] Dorothy Day, *The Long Loneliness: The Autobiography of Dorothy Day* (San Francisco: Harper and Row, 1952), 286.

looking good in the community was important to my parents."
For Elizabeth, religion "felt like social obligations for my parents
and didn't connect directly to anything of value to me, although
the hint of something numinous in the older Catholic churches—
these gorgeous, esoteric buildings themselves—planted a little
seed." That seed would take decades to manifest and would end
up changing her notion of what family might mean. But for most
of her childhood, "I had no belief in something larger than me,
or any understanding of a Creator, Boss, or heavenly Father. That
part was kind of a blank slate until I was older."

As an adolescent Elizabeth dealt with some difficult family
dynamics and began to grapple with depression. "But each time I
was at my lowest, I felt an unseen presence with me that gave me a
sense of being loved. That prevented me from taking my life. That
presence has always driven a lot of my religious seeking—as I've
gotten older, I've chased it, it's chased me, and it's been present
for a lot more pleasant sustaining experiences." She describes this
ongoing sense as "the presence of something that loved me," and
adds that along the way, "I'd found small voices here and there
suggesting I had some agency and some sort of purpose in the
world. These all happened through writings I found or experiences
I had by myself or in one-on-one conversations." However, like
many people raised in families that had been burned by religion,
"the reality of a community of faith was quite foreign to me."

As she got older, Elizabeth also began to question her gender
identity. "I was assigned female at birth," she writes, echoing
many people who struggle with fitting into gender norms. "I was
also a fat kid—and a fat girl—so I got the message that my body
was bad." For a time she joined a neo-Pagan community, something that looked like a family. Some of her Pagan friends began
having conversations about God. That in turn led her to check out
a Unitarian church. "Congregational life was so alien to me. But
Sunday service—with a Buddhist preacher—was centering and
thought provoking. The church did good work helping people and
encouraging personal growth in its members. And the community
was incredibly diverse—even stretching across faith traditions—so
there seemed to be lots of room to be different. I came to love

the denomination the best I knew how, and for the first time, I could picture myself being in a religious vocation." Coming from a marginally Catholic/Protestant background where religion had never been at the forefront of her life, Elizabeth's discovery that seminary might be a possible avenue to pursue was completely unexpected. But that same Presence she'd identified with as a child was exactly what drove her to the Graduate Theological Union (GTU) in Berkeley.

At the GTU Elizabeth discovered that she could, for the first time, "do theology." "The GTU was a huge part" of her discovery of the Christian radical tradition, which has deep roots in Catholicism. "It was steeped in liberation theology, in diverse nonwhite theologies, in anti-colonialism." The interfaith and interdenominational overlapping at the GTU allowed Elizabeth a kind of mystical encounter. "I met God full on as a source of liberation and studied amazing prophets of all kinds." As part of her training to be a hospital chaplain, she was assigned to do research into her family's religious history, and it was in that digging that she discovered the source of their issues with the church. "When I started asking questions, I discovered something terrible and revelatory: one of my parents had been sexually abused by clergy as a child." This shook up Elizabeth's growing consciousness that she, too, was a Christian, deep down. "This revelation really seemed to bring home for me that my whole family history . . . it was all steeped in Christianity, good and bad. The devoted Irish Catholic great-grandmother I never knew, the quieter German Protestant branches . . . my own parents and their complicated relationships with religion . . . it all informed me. It marked me with a certain set of stories that actively claimed me."

"What I learned right then was that Christianity in particular was claiming me. This had been impossible to see when my understanding of Christianity boiled down to televangelists, or the modern culture wars, or even the Apostles' or Nicene Creed." Being steeped in the culture of seminary changed that understanding of Christianity and how it works. "I . . . had been exposed to feminist theologians sweating over texts, exposed to Catholic Workers and congregations of gay people and the desert mystics and process theologians. Once I knew I could find a space, I could face my obligation to make a space."

Elizabeth was ordained as a chaplain in the United Church of Christ (UCC), and went to work for an inner-city hospital. There the politics of faith collided with corporate greed, and the executives of the religiously based organization that bought out the hospital "had dollar signs in their eyes" and decimated the community of long-time staff that, for Elizabeth and the needy people in the community served by the hospital, had become a kind of de facto family. That experience burned her badly enough that she began to seek out other ways to live her faith. "I lost any trust that large-scale human structures could avoid deeply embedding structural oppression. So I stopped looking to them for answers and stopped blessing them with my time. I began to study Christian anarchists and began to look for new ways to relate to people. I now look for smaller ways to connect, to help, to support, to be loving community."

For Elizabeth, as for many of the people who feel marginalized by their faith traditions, seeking a faith community has meant a lot of shopping around. She and her partner have tried out multiple congregations and denominations. Initially, she went back to the UCC, in which she'd been ordained, but the local UCC parish had "a used-car salesman feel from the pastor" that felt "icky." So they tried again. And again. "We tried a congregation affiliated with the Christian Church/Disciples of Christ. The sermons were nourishing, and the building was lovely. We just didn't find a way into connecting socially with the congregation, who leaned quite a bit to the older and conservative side." This made Elizabeth and her partner a bit uncomfortable about being open about their sexuality. "We tried a home church for a while and had a great time with it. It eventually ran its course when my honey and I ran out of steam as the de facto leaders." They've also attended a Quaker meeting, but "we've not yet found that social connection with the small group that meets [many are significantly older], but we enjoy their hospitality very much." They have had a bit more luck with the queer-friendly Metropolitan Community Church, which "is gifted with a truly amazing sense of hospitality," but its pro-capitalist message chafes against their Christian anarchist leanings. "I guess you could say we're hard to please," Elizabeth admits.

However, she continues, "it's not my intention to place myself above anyone or any group. I'm not saying anyone is beneath or not worthy or not Christian enough for us. They're just not offering help with the life we feel Christ calls us to." When I ask if being a Christian without a community is difficult, she replies, "It certainly feels easier to stay true to what I feel my values and Christian path should be by being outside most religious communities I can find. Which is just . . . bizarre to me. I want community. I need community, to be Christian as I understand it."

So, like many Millennials and Gen Xers, Elizabeth and her intentional family have instead found their community online. Twitter, Tumblr, Facebook, and blogs keep them connected to other queer Christians with radical politics and have even enabled Elizabeth to do some mentoring of younger people who have reached out to her online. But it's not a substitute for the kind of social ties her family once had, generations ago, before religion burned them enough to push them away. For now, her Christian faith can only exist in a small community, the community she creates at home. "Maybe I'm a bit like the desert hermits that lived in caves," she says, before signing off on her last email, "just far away from their fellow monks to be alone with God, but close enough to share Eucharist occasionally."

"So, okay. Some family background," Joshua begins. A journalist in Boston, Joshua and I met through mutual friends who'd been involved in the Occupy movement. I knew he was a practicing Buddhist in the Tibetan Buddhist tradition, but more recently we'd also been having conversations about Christianity, and he revealed more than a passing knowledge of Christian tradition—he'd obviously been thinking and reading about Christianity in depth for some time. When he visited the Bay Area for a Buddhist Peace Fellowship meeting of Buddhist political activists, we spent an afternoon talking about religion and writing, and I discovered that he'd recently been attending Episcopal services. However, as it turned out, Joshua had come to this juncture of Buddhist and Episcopalian practice through a different source. He was baptized and partially brought up in the Catholic Church. But, like the religious journeys of many seekers, even that story is complicated.

"I was raised by my mom and grandma mostly," he says on the phone from Boston. "My parents divorced when I was one. I was born in Nashville, which is where my dad's family is settled, but they're actually from Boston." His father's family were "old Unitarian Boston Brahmins," who today are mostly no longer practicing Unitarians. "My mom's side of the family was working class from Georgia, traditionally Methodist. My grandma started going to a Southern Baptist Revival meeting and got religion for a while. But they weren't super religious. They're broadly evangelical, but not hardline by Georgia standards."

Around the time that Joshua was born, his mother converted to Catholicism. "A lot of what she talks about when she talks about conversion is actually that she was way less interested in the theology than the aesthetics. Beauty or the art and liturgy. All the Baptist and Methodist churches down south are very non-liturgical. They look like banks." His mother was drawn to "gorgeous music, organ music," and that was a rarity in southern evangelical churches. So, while living in Tennessee, she converted. "That's where I was christened, at St. Anne's in Nashville."

But the complexities of Southern Christian culture were revealed to Joshua even at a young age. "Growing up, my closest friend was Disciples of Christ," which in the South is loosely a mainline Protestant denomination. "We were in youth group together. I went to parochial school for two years, kindergarten and first grade, and it was just too expensive. Mom wanted me to have some religious education, so she switched me to this supposedly nondenominational Christian school, which in the South means hardline evangelical." Joshua's family had never been strict about its Christianity in the way that his evangelical school was strict: no pants on women, no dancing. And his mother was "naive about it. She didn't realize people were that hardline. She didn't realize how anti-Catholic they were." Joshua attended that school for four years and had Bible study every day. He also repeatedly heard the message that he needed to "get saved" and that infant baptism "didn't count," so he asked his mother if he could get baptized by immersion "because I wanted it to count," he says with a laugh.

Around the time Joshua got to middle school, "the Catholic church was getting really crowded and impersonal. They kept moving priests; every other year there was a new priest." His mother did not react well to this. "So she started going to the Episcopal church down the street," where there was "Eucharist at every service and chasubles, the same liturgy." Joshua says in retrospect that his mother didn't really care or notice the distinctions between the Catholic and Episcopal Churches. "When she converted to Catholicism, she did religious ed. But going to Episcopal Church was just moving churches." By the time he got to high school, "we stopped going to church, or we'd go on Christmas and Easter. Part of that was my mom working a second job on weekends." This lapse in church attendance lasted through most of Joshua's time in high school. At that point he considered himself very loosely Christian. "Maybe with a side of SBNR [spiritual but not religious]. But I wasn't regularly attending a church. And also in high school I had a very superficial cultural interest in Buddhism. But that was just being a hippie," he adds with a laugh, "which I was."

Of his early encounters with Buddhism he points to a teacher in high school "who was kind of both Catholic and Buddhist. He introduced us to a lot of things but was kind of a big intellectual influence on me. He introduced us to beat poets, bebop, jazz, had one of his classes read *Malcolm X*." In the South this was "not normal high school stuff. But he also had us read *Siddhartha,*" the novel by Herman Hesse based on the life of the Buddha. "And we did a little something in English class, a little unit on Buddhism." Around the same time Joshua got a job shelving books at the local library, where he encountered a coworker who identified as a Buddhist.

"I graduated high school in 2002 and went straight to college." He'd attended high school in Athens, a "little liberal island in Georgia." But he attended college at the University of West Georgia in Carleton, near the Alabama border. Carleton was "much more conservative and smaller." What drew him to the school was its psychology program, which "is really unique. It's humanistic transpersonal psychology. A really wacky psych program in an otherwise staid conservative public university." That program, he says, is also the only one at the college that draws students from outside of the immediate geographic area. "Freshman year I got interested in having some sort of spiritual tradition and religious community. And some sort of formal practice. And I was kind of, you know, searching."

Joshua attended Catholic mass "a couple of times," but it proved to be a bad experience. The priest was the Catholic chaplain to the college, and "he was really conservative. He told me that he thought God killed Thomas Merton," a writer Joshua was increasingly starting to identify with, "to keep him from going astray toward Buddhism. He also said that he prayed every night that the United States would find Bin Laden. It was the most pressing thing he could think of, I guess." In retrospect, Joshua says that Catholicism would actually have been a good fit for him at the time. "I think if there'd just been a better priest and community I probably would have stayed in the church. But there wasn't." Later in his life it would be the Catholic writers Dorothy Day and Thomas Merton who helped guide Joshua to his journalistic career. But after the experience with the chaplain, he lost interest, even if Catholicism seemed the best alternative to conservative Southern Christianity. As bad as the campus Catholic church was, for example, it was still the best option for his queer Christian friends, who all attended it. "Everything else was conservative evangelical, much more vocally anti-gay. Even anti-evolution. So if you voted Democrat, the Catholic church was where you went." But Joshua couldn't deal with the weird rantings of the campus chaplain and continued to look around for a different religious community. He was interested in Quakers but discovered there weren't any in that part of Georgia.

After his failed restart with Catholicism, Joshua wound up circling back to his interest in Buddhism. "By total serendipity I had to take a required psych class, and I signed up for the best one for my schedule. It turned out the professor was a Buddhist and taught a Buddhist psychology course." The instructor met with Joshua after class and began recommending reading. "I started reading a lot more, trying to meditate, and that was kind of how I got into it." Joshua was interested both in Zen and Tibetan Buddhism, but since his professor turned out to be in the Tibetan tradition, with "teachers and a lineage and all that stuff," Joshua found himself immersed in Tibetan Buddhist teaching and practice. The summer after his freshman year he took a road trip with a friend and they wound up in Sedona, Arizona, "which happens to have a big Tibetan Buddhist temple next to the public library where we went to check our email." As it turned out, that temple was in the same school of Buddhism as his professor, which Joshua did not know before he made the trip. So, "that was that." By the time he returned to college, more students had become interested in Buddhism, so their professor had taken them on retreat and started a meditation course. That lasted throughout Joshua's undergraduate years.

In the summer of 2005, Joshua temporarily moved into Hadley House, a Catholic Worker house in Boston. "I'd been going to School of the Americas Watch protests in Columbus, Georgia." He says that "there was always a big Catholic Worker presence" at the School of the Americas Watch events. While he'd also been reading Dorothy Day and was starting to feel a pull toward her social justice–oriented faith practice, Joshua "wanted to live in a Worker house that wasn't super Catholic." Hadley House, he says, is "kinda Buddhist. The founder is a Buddhist, and lots of Buddhists go through there." At Hadley House, Joshua "lived in the community, ran the soup kitchen and the clothing closet." The Workers had faith sharing once a week, but rather than being Christo-centric, it was more freeform: "Let's talk about this issue, or let's share faith, or let's do an Enneagram together."

Joshua graduated in 2006 and spent a year back in Athens doing AmeriCorps service work with the homeless. While he'd been at Hadley House, he had started to look into his family history in Boston. His great-grandfather was a Unitarian minister whose papers were collected at Harvard Divinity School. When Joshua went to visit Harvard Divinity School and look through those papers, he noticed a bulletin board for a Buddhist student group. "I thought it was a Christian seminary," he says, "which it isn't. It's very interfaith. So I decided I wanted to apply." At that point he had an unfocused, "amorphous interest in religion and social justice," and seminary seemed like a place where he might bring that amorphous interest into focus.

He applied only to Harvard, with no expectations of being accepted, and got in. After his first year he switched from the master of theological studies program to the master of divinity (MDiv), with plans to pursue a PhD afterward. "As I was filling out the application to switch programs, Lehman Brothers was collapsing, so I wanted to stay in the boat as long as I could." He admits that watching unemployment creep up to 9 percent motivated him to stay in grad school, but as he immersed himself in MDiv studies, other factors began to arise. "Part of it was genuine interest in Buddhist ministry" and helping others to see Buddhism "not just in terms of practice or meditation or philosophy, but how Buddhist communities operate and meet people's needs beyond just meditation or religious instruction." Joshua wanted to understand Buddhist approaches to "pastoral care, physical needs, those sorts of things." He graduated in 2010, still planning on pursuing the PhD. But "nothing about my story is simple," he says in retrospect.

Before he went to college, Joshua had been interested in journalism but had been scared off by "people telling me how cut-throat it is." He helped publish a newsletter in AmeriCorps and became the editor of the Harvard Divinity School newsletter. "I remember at one point I was in 'Intro to Ministry Studies,'" and one of the books the class read was Dorothy Day's *The Long Loneliness*. "That was a really big influence for me. A really big influence." He was assigned an essay on his ministry and how these books he was reading fit into it. Joshua "wasn't on ordination track and didn't have a career path in front of me. So I wrote on writing being my ministry. Even as I was writing, I was scared off. I thought, no one makes a living at this." His plan was to pursue the PhD, become a professor, and do public intellectual work "on the side," because he "wanted to be inside an institution that would take care of my basic needs, and I was naive enough to think that was academia." When he graduated in 2010, he "foundered for a long time." A combination of temporary jobs, editing gigs, and sleeping in friend's spare rooms was barely sustainable as a lifestyle. "I'm not even sure how I made ends meet." This itinerant pattern lasted until 2012.

In the midst of his postgraduate foundering, "Occupy happened. It was a huge thing" for Joshua and "for everyone who was involved. It changed our lives." Joshua was on the media team for Occupy Boston, where he learned how to do live tweeting and live streaming, and was "making connections with people who were journalists or who became them, especially lefty journalists on Twitter." At the same time he was dating a woman doing an internship in Ottawa, Canada, and was finishing his PhD applications. Eventually, he applied to five schools, and was accepted at UC Santa Barbara (UCSB). But UCSB only offered partial funding, and Joshua "couldn't go without funding. I didn't want more debt for a PhD in religious studies." Around the same time he and his girlfriend broke up. And "Occupy Boston finally fell apart. All those things fell apart at once."

In response to the termination of his relationship, the collapse of Occupy, and the end of his plans for graduate school, Joshua finally circled back to the idea he'd had during his MDiv—that writing could be his ministry. After turning down the offer from UCSB, "I decided not to reapply to PhD [programs] and I had to figure out another way. I just finally said, let me try this journalism thing." A former divinity-school colleague contacted him with a lead on a job at *Spare Change News,* a street newspaper run by the Homeless Empowerment Project. Joshua became the paper's web editor. Late in 2012, "self-immolations in Tibet were spiking. I had a degree in Tibetan Buddhist studies from Harvard, so I started pitching" stories to editors about the self-immolations, many of which were being done by Buddhist monks. "There was a kind of synchronicity" to this series of events. "I'd been banging my head against the wall, and suddenly, as soon as I started writing, things started clicking." Joshua's reporting on Tibet led to stories in Al Jazeera's English-language edition, where he later began reporting on Edward Snowden and the NSA leaks. Some of this was "blind luck and privilege." But "it also seemed like things were working out." Suddenly, journalism seemed like a real career, and one that finally brought together his activism and faith journey. He began to think that "maybe this is what I was meant to be doing."

In the midst of finally finding his way to a career, however, the wheels guiding his faith life began to fall off. Right now, Joshua says that he "goes to an Episcopal church irregularly. I used to be very clear that I was a Buddhist, and now I'm not. It's distressing and also weird. I feel like an ambulance with its sirens blaring. I start praying to Tara," a female manifestation of Buddha, "and then start saying Hail Marys, and I don't know what to do." In divinity school there was a culture of trying to pursue an authentic Tibetan Buddhist identity. But that culture, to Joshua, seems "kind of macho, uptight, super intellectualized. And in a way, after being in that, it's nice to hold these identities kind of loosely. It's kind of a relief." These days he feels less tied up in trying to "assert, defend, or authenticate" his Buddhism. He says he is neither trying to be "a great Buddhist practitioner or a great Christian." For now, "it feels nice to kind of lean into the uncertainty and indeterminacy of not really knowing. And kind of trying to give up that need to feel in control of things."

"My writing for a long time was really focused on politically engaged Buddhism." More recently, the Buddhist Peace Fellowship, an activist group he's involved with, has begun to take off, and Joshua feels relief that he's no longer "banging my head against the wall and getting nowhere and getting no response from people" when it comes to expecting and hoping for more activism from the Buddhist community. In the past he sometimes felt "a little bit alone in my concerns" that American Buddhists could be too focused on inward-looking spirituality and had lost the opportunity to do outreach in the manner he'd witnessed at School of the Americas or Hadley House.

But Joshua's faith in his Buddhist community had also been tested and challenged by cross-cultural notions of the role Buddhism should play in America. "In Tibet," he says, "Buddhism is much more integrated into everyday life, into community and society. There are folk practices that mark seasons of the year, stages of life, and rites of passage. Communities have ways of providing what we might call pastoral care and social services. Tibetans themselves sometimes make a distinction between *mi chos* (the religion of people) and *lha chos* (the religion of gods). When Buddhism came to the United States, it was brought by lamas who were primarily interested in preserving *lha chos*— the high philosophical teachings and advanced contemplative practices that were studied and practiced in monasteries. That means Westerners missed out on everything that was rooted in community and family, all of the *mi chos*. Most Tibetan Buddhist groups in the United States are still structurally ill-equipped to provide that kind of community and support. It's not that people are cold or uncaring," he adds, "it's just not how these groups are set up."

After graduating, during his spate of under-employment, Joshua went into "a bad depression." His Buddhist community at that point was very spread out, with its monastery based in upstate New York; Joshua had lived there "a couple of times." When things got emotionally challenging, he "reached out to them," but it proved difficult to get a response. The combination of these things began to put distance between Joshua and what he'd worked to build up as a Buddhist identity. "I had these intellectual problems and differences" with Tibetan Buddhism, "but I also felt this personal loss" when the community couldn't respond to him.

Joshua says he's still searching for a spiritual community. He repeats the phrase "that's a loss" several times when talking about his recent distance from Buddhism. And he also feels a growing sense that he needs to reconnect with his Christian roots. "When I exclusively identified as a Tibetan Buddhist and I'd go to a service at the divinity school and hear great hymns or see a beautiful icon in a church, I'd feel like, ahhhh, I miss this." The longing is "about Buddhism now." So, rather than trying to belong to, claim, or identify with one or the other, Joshua is somewhere in between. According to Joshua, "you can't necessarily have both." For now, he's redirected his focus from practice to consciousness. Instead of committing to one faith or the other, he tries to maintain his "emotional connection."

But is that emotional connection enough to sustain a person's idea of faith if the community fails him or her? Baptism, after all, is considered in most Christian traditions to be enough to connect a person to religion for a lifetime. Confirmation, if a person bothers to go through with it, is both in the Anglican communion and in Catholicism a strange notion; it is supposed to bring people closer to their faith as an adult choice, and yet most people go through it when they're about twelve years old, which is not exactly the age of wisdom. Even adults confirmed into one Christian religion or another may wonder what the purpose of saying those words might really be. In Judaism, when a person goes through the bat mitzvah or bar mitzvah, she or he writes a "drash," breaking down the meaning of the Torah portion for the congregation. Christians stand up and recite a script. Does that bring them more deeply into the community? Does it create lasting ties? It depends on the individual, but in a greater sense, it is not so much a ritual of claiming one's faith by demonstrating one's understanding of it, but a ritual of asking to be accepted by others. Sometimes that acceptance is more gestural than anything else.

The idea of cultural Catholicism takes on a very abstract meaning today, especially for people like Joshua and Elizabeth, whose ties to Catholicism are, at best, loose. When Dana Gioia uses the phrase, he is referring to ways of life that are fading away for many younger people: the bonds of religion and tribe that were based on being surrounded by others who believed in the same things you and everyone in your family believed. For many Americans that notion is two or three generations in the past. If religion is becoming a choice rather than something handed down, that means that the things it once brought to people, like ties and community, will also become communities of choice rather than default ones based on a semblance of belief. What those communities will look like, for Elizabeth and Joshua, remains unclear.

Ties and community, after all, take time to develop. But our culture is impatient, and many of us are picky individuals who have been brought up to know what we want. Younger people are used to being able to customize things: computers, phones, groups of friends . . . these are a series of choices resulting in something that resembles the person who assembled it. It may seem trivial to compare faith to this, but in many ways, when we break off from the faith of our families and try to create a faith of our own, we too are picking and choosing and reassembling the old into something new. We are customizing our faith and looking for others who might like to do the same. We are looking for people to create something different along with us. You might even call it a transfiguration.

10

The Binding

"The true vocation story has a lot do to with my sense of deep unsettlement," Kyle tells me through a twitchy Skype connection. Bearish and in his thirties, Kyle and I were introduced by mutual friends who told me he had a complex relationship with Catholicism. That complexity, as it turned out, involved trying to be a priest when he wasn't even sure if there was a God. Kyle's accent immediately gives away his Cajun roots, but the South plays an even deeper part in his religious identity than the sonic qualities of speech might initially reveal. "The South is a very weird place. Deep misogyny and backwardness wrapped in the worship of tradition and family—very Tennessee Williams. A veneer of severe dysfunction." By the time he was in his twenties, Kyle "knew I wanted out, and I knew I wanted to do something radical. Talking with friends, reading 'fring-y' things by clerics, Jesuits kept appearing. On a lark, I applied; I didn't think they'd take me."

They did. "I entered the Society of Jesus at twenty-one after graduating from Louisiana State University," he continues. "We were shuffled around, doused in the ministries." Kyle had an early suspicion that the Jesuit idea of vocation to the priesthood—being called by God to an itinerant ministry and life in community—might not have matched up with the tangled story of how he wound up as a Jesuit. "I have a real dislike for teenagers," he admits, but during Jesuit formation he "was sent to a high school and told to give my vocation story. There's no quicker way to lose a vocation than to tell the story a hundred times." So, like the Southern Catholic writers he often refers to as part of his religious evolution, Kyle found a creative method for dealing with the problem. "I fudged the story," he admits.

When I ask about his real vocation story, it unfolds in an unexpected way. Most priests talk about a persistent call from God, rather like a nagging grandmother who telephones at the most inconvenient moments. Kyle, on the other hand, talks about being driven into the priesthood by doubt. "I have a real distinct experience that's the core of what I believe. Being fourteen or fifteen and coming to understand my weirdness in relation to the place I grew up. Small town, everyone's Catholic. Lying in my bed one night, I was taken by this darkness above me. This concept came to me that fundamentally, I am alone. Just me and a cycle of light and darkness. The great burden that is time. What to fill it with is the question. That's still what I fundamentally think about God."

With this vision of God as a kind of unfillable void, Kyle nonetheless felt pulled to join a religious community. But this required a reinvention of his core identity. "To be part of a religious order I couldn't have that kind of atheism," he admits. "So I was cloaking myself in the spiritual but not religious. I'd reverse that. I'm religious in the sense of binding, seeking community." Kyle was baptized a Catholic but didn't regularly attend church, which he refers to as a "Cajun social phenomenon." Instead of being formed from the inside out, his Catholicism came from the outside in. "I became a Catholic as a Jesuit." Jesuit formation "came to help me appreciate the figure of Jesus—I mean the literary Jesus." His Jesus, he says, was something like the character of Ignatius J. Reilly in John Kennedy Toole's novel *A Confederacy of Dunces*—a man at odds with the world he lives in. The title of Toole's novel is from Jonathan Swift's essay "Thoughts on Various Subjects, Moral and Diverting": 'When a true genius appears in the world," Swift writes, "you may know him by this sign; that the dunces are all in confederacy against him."[1] That man became Kyle's Jesus.

---

[1] John Kennedy Toole, *A Confederacy of Dunces* (Louisiana State University Press, 1980). Jonathan Swift, "Thoughts on Various Subjects, Moral

As to why he picked the Jesuits, Kyle says that even if he had doubts about God, "you can't help but be taken by good theism. That's what drew me—the stories of the early Jesuits." The missionary saint "Francis Xavier is deeply concerned about these people who he has no reason to be concerned about." Kyle was seduced by the idea of experiencing "that depth of feeling—concern for someone who is not your family or friend to the point that you'll learn their language, take on their clothing, be willing to stay in Japan." To become a Jesuit, he says, "you will start from the top down." At that juncture in his life, radical self-sacrifice of the kind a missionary religious order requires was "this really foreign concept to me. Loving people as you love yourself. That's a hard teaching, but it really captured me." And the historical juncture at which he entered the Jesuits was part of the puzzle of trying to get closer to something that might offer the world some sense of healing. "This is 2001. The hole in New York is still smoldering. Nothing is pointing to love or compassion except this thing." "This thing," for Kyle, was religious life.

Kyle spent five years in the Jesuits. When he left, he persisted in pursuing a life as a priest. "I went into the diocesan seminary for one and a half years," and that's when thing fell apart. "That experience gave me a better sense of how unique the Jesuits were. In a more conventional program priests are expected just to survive. Bishops are only concerned with the need for bodies." The diocesan seminarians spent a relatively short time in formation, compared to the decade or more it takes to become a Jesuit. In the diocese "guys are made pastor after one year. It was a completely vacant academic environment." He for the first time ran up against the rampant clericalism that often underlies American religious life. And he also came to terms with Catholicism's Janus-faced attitude toward gay men in the clergy.

"There was a director of human formation" in Kyle's diocesan seminary who wound up being the catalyst for his departure from

---

and Diverting," in *The Battle of the Books and Other Short Pieces* (London: Cassell, 1886; the essay was originally published in 1727), available online at http://www.gutenberg.org/files/623/623–h/623–h.htm.

religious life. "He was mostly concerned about masturbation. It was creepy." Diocesan seminary also presented a problem for something that hadn't been much of an issue in the Jesuits. "I was comfortable being queer in the Society but never in the diocesan seminary."

Kyle wound up writing "this milquetoast paper about incorporating LGBTQ people in a parish. The first thing I got in response was 'why would you write this?'" The formation director pushed the paper at Kyle across his desk, saying "I don't understand why someone would write a paper about gay people." The meeting continued, and "by the end of the conversation he's got a list of things to say. And he says I don't bow properly when I pass priests in the hallway." Clericalism had finally drawn the line. "And I just said, 'I'm going to go now.'" And he did.

Once he left the seminary, Kyle went through a long period of trying to understand his relationship to the open question of faith. Forcing himself into the identity of a Catholic priest when his doubts ran deep had proved to be a bad fit, but once he left, there were no easy answers about where those lingering questions about God might take him. "There was a certain cocooning from twenty-one to twenty-eight in this spiritual realm." But throughout that time he felt a "deep skepticism about the nature of life. In the Jesuits there are the virtues that draw us out of ourselves. Diocesan seminary was a more strident theism. As I go through these layers, I'm so far from what I believe. What sort of agnostic says 'I should go be a priest?'" Once he was out of religious life, "there was some despair about wasting my life and understanding why I should do what I don't believe. There was a sense of liberation, but also a profound loneliness, an odd imposition."

When I ask where Kyle finds himself now in relation to faith, he describes a "tractor-beam Catholicism" that hasn't entirely left him, a "deeply mystical, ethnocentric Catholicism. In 2009 I tried to push that out. But I recognize more and more that's a futile effort. I've always been fascinated by love, and that's become my central tenet. The thing that's opened me up to that has been fiction. I was introduced to Walker Percy after the seminary. I really appreciate Southern writers' understanding of meaningful people as odd people. They're just weirdos. There's no other religious traditions that embrace weirdness like Catholicism." Kyle has also begun to wonder what he can draw from religious communities outside the church. "Something else unaccounted for in seminary was interreligious experience." At this moment in time he doesn't have "a Catholic community. But I can find that in Unitarians, Buddhists, Ba'hai's. That's the bridge that keeps me from going insane. This Christ-haunted body I possess doesn't have to be haunted by ancestral Catholicism."

As to why he persists in the search for binding, for ties in a faith community, Kyle says that "the draw of those communities is praxis. I've had enough of doctrine and creeds." At this point in his life "more things fall on personal choice." When it comes to talking about religion, "it's not a 'convincible' conversation. I don't want to have those conversations any more. I want to find common ground." Instead of looking for a way to believe, Kyle is more interested now in ways to interact. "In ways, our lives as people of consciousness give us a way to live. I've come to my own conclusions about dogma, and they don't fit, and I don't care." Even though he doesn't like saying he believes in God, "I'd still call myself a Catholic." After Kyle left the seminary, he picked up a book by the Anglican bishop John A. T. Robinson called *Honest to God.* "That book was a great help in developing encounter. That's why I don't fear calling myself a Catholic. We get really involved in fictional characters all the time, and we'd be stupid to act like literary figures aren't needed to be human. The figure of God is an important character in my attempt to be human."

Several months later we connect on Skype again, prompted by our mutual decision that maybe we need to go deeper into the question of "God stuff" and the Catholic Church. Kyle is a political consultant and was at that point on the campaign trail with a Southern Democratic senator. Maybe it was Kyle's immersion in political life, but our conversation quickly pivots to issues of generation gaps and their influence on religious views among younger people. When I ask Kyle to talk more about how he relates to the idea of God today, he says that "a lot of things are products of your raising. You engage with the culture of your parents. My parents are Boomers, and a reason the Nones exist is because a lot of us had nonreligious parents. They wouldn't call themselves atheists or nonbelievers. I grew up in a nonreligious house. When I went to college, I met seriously religious people."

The Jesuits were a catalyst for thinking about God in a different way. "In the Society you put on a certain armor." At that point in time "I probably had those nonreligious views but adopted that language. I never talked to God or Jesus. What offered me another conversation piece was Ignatian contemplation." Kyle found that Ignatian contemplation, the process of imagining yourself into Bible stories, was, for him, "like reading a novel." But after he tried it, and "this was the first time I was able to articulate a God-language."

Eventually, however, that fell away. "In the end," Kyle says, God is "all imagination. On the question of who God is, who cares? So what's the value of God? The value is in religion in the old sense, is in the binding." But, he adds, there's still a divide between child and parent when it comes to understanding religion. For Kyle, this mirrors the gaping holes in the social structure. "[The Boomers] slid in on the backs of the Greatest Generation. They abused the social safety net and pulled the ladder up behind them."

In a similar context, he adds, this disinterest in the future led to "Millennials reaching their thirties leaving behind organized religion or embracing what I call plural religion. Boomers say that's not how you do it. But they gave us open-mindedness," resulting in a sense of frustration among younger people who feel they're working with mixed messages about religion from Boomer parents, who may freak out over their children leaving religion but also stress individuality as the route to happiness rather than modeling community ties. "Millennials are less religious" than previous generations, "but we also don't care or don't have a burning desire to tell people what to do. Boomers are moralistic, but their morals change with age." For Kyle, that adds up to him having to make his own decisions. "The best part of that is encountering religion for myself instead of their telling me who God is.

Communal life, how God is animating someone in the moment. That's a God I can care about."

Kyle sees Boomers' mixed messages as the root of many problems with institutional Catholicism. "Boomer Catholics are bitter about the new creed," he says, referring to the changes in the language of the prayers that sent a wave of angry chatter through many American parishes in 2011. And the more conservative leanings of a younger generation of priests who came into the church during the papacies of John Paul II and Benedict further reveal what looks like an unbridgeable generation gap in the church. Of his time in the seminary, Kyle says, "I entered with a class where maybe ten [seminarians] were into the Latin mass. The older guys—it killed them that these were the people who wanted religious life. But, that always happens after a council because of the upheaval." In other words, after the upheaval, the backlash.

But Kyle also senses a deeper struggle between generations of Catholics. "Something different in America is that Catholicism is of zero relevance to anybody." After the sex scandals were exposed, "people have a legitimate grievance against the church." When Kyle entered the priesthood, "Boston was at its height," putting the spotlight on priests "who raped children for thirty years" and on bishops who covered it up. Kyle recalls that the former Archbishop of San Francisco, John Quinn, "at that point said priesthood had no value. But the reality is that for those of us who attempt to wander" from Catholicism, "we don't take it extremely seriously. We don't have that respect for the church, and some don't know how to form a community."

All of this leaves Kyle with some open-ended questions. While he still feels pulled to Catholicism and still identifies as Catholic, he also sees himself increasingly isolated from the same sort of religious community that drew him to Catholicism in the first place. "Gay men are the products of their environment. But I see that with religion too. As a theological progressive I'm a community of one. I'm surrounded by traditionalists or people who see Catholicism as vestigial. But neither group is interested in being a seeker." He rattles off the names of a few progressive Catholic organizations that in the past had provided some kind of structure and community for Catholics on the fringes and asks, "Where are they today? What does it mean today? I have no idea how to go about being what I am today."

Conversations with Kyle led to more questions about the evolving identity of young Catholics who lacked deep ties to the church, who knew about the implications of Vatican II, but who had grown up with the backlash that followed in its wake. Was Catholicism about practice and ritual more than belief? Was it really about constructing ties that would be enough to sustain a person through the loss of a priest, a parish, or a family that drifted away from the church?

For Kyle, and also for Maria, who was raised Catholic and still identifies as Catholic even though she no longer attends mass, the binding that religion creates is hard to shake off, even if the church's rigidity makes the experience of being in a congregation too discomforting to attempt very often. If a bishop or priest pushes the focus of a congregation in a singular direction, he risks alienating the very people the church needs most: the socially engaged, informed, thoughtful individuals who see through the veneer of brocade and gilded chalices to the core message of solidarity with the poor and marginalized beneath. Kyle and Maria aren't lapsed Catholics or ex-Catholics—they are more like Catholics in exile.

Maria lives in an East Coast city and is in her mid-thirties. She works in labor organizing, where she sees the focus of her efforts as trying to help the poorest workers "lift themselves out of poverty." Prior to her work in labor, Maria worked at a rape crisis center and as an advocate for LGBTQ rights. Social justice had long formed the core of her identity, and it is directly rooted in her experiences as a Catholic. But some years ago she stopped attending mass.

"I grew up Catholic," she says over the phone. Baptism, first communion, and confirmation were all significant milestones in her childhood. In college Maria became "very involved" at her school's Newman Center, where she was a eucharistic minister and did several mission trips. "A lot of the activism I did growing up and throughout college was around two things. Poverty was a focus of a lot of the work we did." She also studied methods for "creating a better cultural understanding of how poverty comes about, how polices of the United States affect poverty in other countries outside of America." The Newman Center at her college sponsored a trip to Cuernavaca, Mexico, where the Catholic students learned about intercultural development and "global poverty and America's role in that." They also worked with the Franciscan Sisters and traveled to San Francisco's Mission District "to work on an understanding of homelessness and getting a broader understanding of urban homelessness." Maria reiterates that this formation was part and parcel of her Catholic identity. Even today, she says, "the work I do is driven by the church's activism."

After college Maria moved to a new area that she "thought was going to be larger and more progressive. I was surprised to find Catholic churches were very much not in line with my growing up understanding of my Catholic background." Specifically, she noticed that the content of the homilies at masses sounded quite different from what she'd become used to hearing. "I was really surprised they only superficially addressed poverty and inequality and were focused on abortion and same-sex marriage. It was so weird and such a contrast to focus on prayer. In college we focused on prayer and inequality. Prayer after college was specifically on pro-life issues. Not even talking about the death penalty or anti-war messages, just abortion."

With that relentlessly one-sided focus coming from the priests in her new diocese, Maria started to discern whether she really belonged in the Catholic Church any more. "So that was really a moment of trying to reflect on how church doesn't align" with the values she'd understood it to represent. "There was a transition in the church, broadly speaking. It wasn't talking about issues of inequality and poverty. It was more aggressively promoting a different agenda of where resources should be directed." For Maria, this led to a period of "coming to terms with my own personal identity." For a time she attempted "going to church meetings and trying to be involved, but you're getting a message that you don't belong here." Mass became a place of tension. "It wasn't that open place I'd been given in college," she says. She no longer recognized the path of social justice in a broader sense that she'd once understood to be central to her religious identity. The faith she'd belonged to was caught up in the culture wars. "What I'd grown up in was being pushed aside."

At this juncture Maria says that it's probably been "at least three or four years since I've been to church." She chose not to turn to a different Christian religion, as many disgruntled Catholics have. Her Catholicism is too deeply rooted for her to let it go. "I've experimented with other faiths, and I'm searching for a faith home where I can feel comfortable and have a life. But it's tricky trying to find a space like that. It's hard to let go of the Catholic identity." Part of Maria's conflict is that she and her partner, who also grew up Catholic, are both Hispanic. Both come from deeply Catholic families. "It's tough for us to move past that," Maria says, "and find a spiritual home."

When I ask what it feels like making the decision to stop attending church, Maria replies that it's "very much a loss. My parents go to church every Sunday, and I talk to my mom all the time. I ask how mass was, what the homily was about. I still talk to my mom openly about what's going on with the church." Maria is out to her family, and it's begun to cause a rift between her mother and the church as well. "She'll tell me the priest softened the LGBTQ message after Pope Francis," Maria says of her mother, but then, "the priest at her local parish gave a series of homilies about how being a gay person is wrong." Maria says this makes Catholicism "hard for my mom too. She's starting to question" what she hears in church, "because of me and my partner."

Even after a few years away Maria reiterates that "it's hard" because she "misses mass." In an attempt to fill the void she has tried to turn her focus to the work that her faith life initially brought her to. "So much of practicing my beliefs is in the work I do and the life I've led. Trying to be in service to others and broaden my perspectives of the world around me. Being in service to others in the work I do professionally and as a volunteer. Serving others.

That's how I practice my faith in my daily life in terms of the work that I do." Nonetheless, for Maria, no matter how much she tries to embody those Christlike values, feeling rejected by the church is still an absence. "I miss that ability to go and pray with others and feel welcome to be there."

Given her reiteration of how much she misses mass and having a faith community, I ask Maria what it would take for her to go back and start attending church again. "I think it would require a pretty big shift in the church as a whole." For Maria, the overwhelming social issues with inequality are "such a major driving factor in hunger poverty and homelessness. Inequality is at its peak. It's starting to be addressed with Pope Francis, but that message hasn't filtered down through the hierarchy. You still have local parishes preaching about the ills of abortion and the LGBT community." Maria sees the problem with the relentless focus on abortion as especially problematic, because it equates to a narrow definition of what "pro-life" really means. "Even with the pro-life stuff," she says, it's not focused "on a broader understanding of being against the death penalty and war, and understanding issues around that, and what it means to be alive and have a life in this world. You can't separate the two to have a culture of life."

Her sexual orientation remains a major issue in Maria's being able to reconcile with Catholicism. "To be welcomed would be hard with my partner. It would be hard to have to hide something that's so important to my daily life." Even if her own family has become open to her relationship, not being able to "worship with my wife and have the sacraments because [the church] doesn't recognize my wife or that I have one" has continued to push Maria away. Maria and her wife have instead tried to keep Catholicism present in their lives by giving it a prominent place in their home. They are trying to "hold on to a lot of traditional things and bringing the cultural identity aspect of it into our own home. We have a lot of Catholic art in our house; it's a big piece of our cultural identity." That means "providing a place of honor" for the traditional Catholic art they display.

Maria also channels her spiritual life into interfaith work in labor organizing. "I've had the honor of getting to work with some amazing faith leaders" through an organization that's involved in worker's rights issues. "It involved Catholics, Baptists, Unitarians, rabbis, and imams who are all involved in what they're calling the Love Thy Neighbor campaign." Maria has been working with these local faith leaders "to educate the faith-based community about why from a faith perspective the issue of workers being able to support their families and have a livable wage is a fundamental issue and why that's important. For me, that's been helpful in my own journey in understanding the role of faith in our lives." And that's led to more outreach, "supporting labor movements throughout our country in terms of folks who are . . . low-wage workers who haven't had a voice, and are finding their voices." Maria sees issues of labor and fair wages as part and parcel of how working-class people can work together to lift one another out of poverty. Part of the change "is through their faith and spirituality and connections. Being able to work with the faith groups and creating a better understanding of organizing is a big part of raising up those critical issues. There's a faith driven process to it."

Nonetheless, for all of Maria's faith-based outreach work and her attempts to stay connected to Catholicism, she still feels alienated by the institutional church. We wind up our conversation talking about some of the other ways of "being church" that we've both witnessed: the grassroots movements to make a more inclusive space for people like Maria and her wife, the shift back to bigger issues of poverty and the problematic nature of capitalism, priests who are willing to walk alongside their congregations rather than leading them from the top down. But change, we both know, is slow and takes so long to filter down to the average parish that, for some people, it is better to step back and wait it out rather than risk being told that the way God made you is somehow incorrect. "It's hard to go and hear the priest say because of who you are that you're not welcome," she says, just before we say goodbye. "It's tough to know how to feel comfortable in that situation and how to create a spiritual connection."

∽

Maria and Kyle were alienated by the church that still resonated deeply in their souls, as it did for so many others: the childless, the single, the unmarried couples, the divorced, the lapsed, the returned, the doubters, the seekers, the exiled. And those millions of souls? They still wanted what church should have provided: community, consolation, the palpable presence of God. When they were told they didn't fit in, they may have stopped attending mass or changed the way they practiced their faith, but they still felt, and identified, as Catholics.

At base, the church's social messages about care for the most marginalized are what wound up guiding both of them in their careers. For Maria, that means devoting her life to the people on the margins. For Kyle, it means working to create change in government that will benefit those who are most often neglected in society. And that is the emphasis of most Catholic social teaching. So, even though Kyle and Maria were exiled, they were still a part of the church. They wanted the binding. So rather than waiting around, they became DIY church, for a DIY generation, in a time of DIY religion.

11

Guerrilla Faith

Candace Chellew-Hodge, who teaches comparative religion at a community college to mostly Millennial students, gave her class an unusual assignment. She asked them to create their own religion. Although they were initially skeptical ("Isn't that blasphemy?" one asked), they got into groups and made some decisions. Most "incorporated Eastern religious ideas like meditation. When Western religions were included," Chellew-Hodge writes, "the pieces taken from them were such things as pilgrimage . . . or rituals like prayer." What the students were not interested in was authority or dogma. "There were several components of religion that were glaringly absent. Not one of them had career clergy who were in charge of services, rituals, or care of the congregation. There were, for the most part, no regular meetings of the faithful." Not one of her students wanted to create a religion with any version of hell or punishment. "We don't need some church telling us what to do when they don't practice what they preach,"[1] one of her students explained.

Chellew-Hodge admits that this idealized version of religion is missing a significant element: it fails to address the question of why human suffering exists. "By ignoring the question of the suffering of humanity and the role of religion in addressing that suffering," she writes, "I am afraid that this new generation is

---

[1] Candace Chellew-Hodge, "Millennials Invent New Religion: No Hell, No Priests, No Punishment," *Religion Dispatches,* January 29, 2014.

denying itself the opportunity to truly connect not just with the divine, if that's their thing, but with each other."

In *Belief without Borders* scholar and Presbyterian minister Linda Mercadante mainly explores the spiritual lives of the "spiritual but not religious" members of the Boomer generation, but she points to a fact that applies to younger people as well. Without the structure of organized religion, spiritual seekers may end up focusing more on the self than on questions of humanity and community. But that inward turning, like the fantasy religions invented by Chellew-Hodge's students that focus only on meditation and pilgrimage rather than problem-solving tools, may reflect a larger cultural problem. We are increasingly leading lives so scattered that we constantly have to patch ourselves back together again. An inward-seeking spiritual life, Mercadante admits, may simply be a way of "carving out some space away from the distracting, fragmented external world."[2]

Confession: in the time it took me to write those two paragraphs, I checked Twitter four times and Facebook twice, deleted several junk emails, and looked up Mercadante's book online to save the time of finding it on the bookshelf (however, I really did read it in paper). Across the room my husband was watching YouTube clips, and in another room my iPhone was vibrating with text messages. Even in the midst of writing about what has happened to our contemporary notions about faith, doubt, and the role religion will or won't play in resolving the doubt of two very doubt-addled generations, distractions were everywhere around me. But so were solutions.

On Twitter I keep a growing, interfaith list of religion writers, editors, theologians, clergy, seminary students, and other people who believe or don't (the list includes atheists and agnostics who think and write about faith issues). It's called God Etc. When I'm working on an essay or a book, some of my best resources have come from posing queries there or on Facebook. People post articles, questions, and points, and debate them, sometimes falling

---

[2] Linda A. Mercadante, *Belief without Borders: Inside the Minds of the Spiritual but Not Religious* (New York: Oxford University Press, 2014), 236.

into trolling or finger pointing, but far more often providing the closest thing I have to a community of people who are interested in picking apart questions of what we might think of as faith. It is a community without a name, other than the silly one I gave it when prompted to do so. It has no geographic center, although it seems to be more heavily clustered on the East rather than the West Coast. It changes daily, depending on the time of year, the time of day, or the mood the world might happen to be in. But for me and many other people who cannot leave paying jobs to spend several years in graduate school studying religion, or attend seminary, or travel to conferences more than once in a while, the Internet provides a meeting place and has led to multiple conversations about faith issues that can eventually turn into real-world friendships. When church life is disappointing, bland, or unfriendly, something more interesting and meaningful is usually happening online. Sometimes, it is a more willful act not to look at my iPhone during mass than it is to show up in the first place.

This kind of curating of religion that the Internet has opened up is not new. For generations, splits in the Christian faith have meant that there are many, many Protestant denominations to choose from. High or low, traditional or "emergent," they may share tenets at the core, but people decide whether they are getting what they want out of that particular denomination. A young Presbyterian minister I had lunch with admitted that within a few decades her denomination would most likely merge with one of the other mainline Protestant ones that is shrinking in America. This didn't seem to bother her; rather, she saw it a hopeful thing. Perhaps something new would arise out of the old, and she would play a role in shaping it. Similarly, a young rabbi said that the increasing number of secular Jews among the young didn't trouble her too much; Jewish identity, after all, is about more than just attending a synagogue on a regular basis. Muslims have a more structured prayer life than many other religions if they choose to follow the edict to pray five times daily; however, some Muslims, like a writer I know, may identify with Islam and pray to Allah even if they don't attend mosque. Each of these women came to an informed decision about religion on her own. Family, culture, class, education and geographic location played roles in those decisions, but even if they consider themselves religious, that religion shifts and changes daily.

For Catholics, too, there are choices to be made about what kind of Catholic to be. Our Catholicism, in spite of the many pages of catechism we can refer to, is increasingly one that we shape ourselves. Most of the Catholics I interact with, online and in person, would fall into the liberal/progressive Catholic category. This is unsurprising given where I live, where I teach, the magazines I write for, and the books I've written. When my path intersects with more traditionalist Catholics, we can be polite and perhaps learn from one another, but more often, they arrive in my life through comment boxes on online articles or social media, where they tend to be critical (and saying they are merely critical is my attempt at being kind). Fair enough. The Catholic Left, such as it is, can be guilty of the same thing. But among all the younger Catholics I spoke to for this book, whether they were lapsed, practicing, reverts, cultural, or some combination of those categories, there was always some discussion about what the church could or should be. *If* and *when* were commonly used words. Each had some sort of vision of his or her ideal Catholic church. That is something we have in common with our traditionalist Catholic peers, for they too envision what the church "should" be rather than looking at what it is: messy, sprawling, massive, and difficult to define, in spite of its centuries of self-definition.

In some ways evangelicals are ahead of any other religious group when it comes to redefining and recreating the idea of church in a customizable manner that appeals to disenfranchised young adults. Although the phrasing "emergent church" was first used by the Catholic theologian Johann Baptist Metz in 1981, subsequently it's been mostly used by evangelicals as a catch-all for a wide group of forms of worship. Nondenominational Christian churches have their obvious problems; the implosion of Mark Driscoll's hipster-garbed but deeply theologically conservative Mars Hill mega-church is testimony to that. Prior to the series of problems that later broke up Mars Hill, Driscoll's charismatic persona had enabled him to build a church from the ground up.

Mars Hill was founded in 1996, when Driscoll was only twenty-seven. Its first meetings took place in "house churches"; living rooms were where the seeds were planted. From the beginning he described Mars Hill as a "postmodern ministry" aimed at Gen Xers and Millennials who didn't like traditional services.[3] These postmodern churches, Lori Leibovitch wrote in 1998, "are ingeniously adding an anti-establishment spirit to their movement."[4]

Like the mega-churches that came before them, emergent Christian churches foster small groups and community networking. A friend who attended Rick Warren's Saddleback Church in Orange County said that even if the services were packed with thousands of attendants, Saddleback's staff went out of its way to identify and welcome newcomers and introduce them to the range of activities available for all generations, from pickup basketball to infant care to knitting groups. There was a coffee shop in the lobby. Unlike the fantasy religions mentioned by Chellew-Hodge's students, however, even the most hipster-garbed evangelical church has something many younger people are wary of: a pastor who determines the style and direction of worship and belief. But because nondenominational churches have no structured form of service, they embody some of that DIY spirit people long for in these post-religious times.

"Church planting" has become an evangelical way of life; there are thousands of nondenominational Christian churches meeting in shopping malls, nightclubs, living rooms, college dormitories, public parks, and almost anywhere else that people could possibly gather

---

[3] Brendan Kiley's 2012 exposé of Mars Hill in the Seattle free weekly *The Stranger* ripped the lid off of a particularly nasty can of worms. Driscoll, for all of his emphasis on services that looked like a rock concert, had "molded a doctrine based on manliness, sexual purity, and submission to authority: wives to husbands, husbands to pastors, and everyone to God." People who disagreed with leaders at Mars Hill were told they were being "insubordinate" when they refused to "submit." Those who left the church were told to cut all ties to friends and family who remained members. With these kinds of problems finally being aired, the church's dissolution a few years later wasn't entirely surprising.

[4] Lori Leibovich. "Generation: A Look inside Fundamentalism's Answer to MTV: The Postmodern Church," *Mother Jones* (July/August 1998).

aside from an actual church building. (However, some Mainline Protestant churches are beginning to rent their space to emergent churches when they're not hosting a regular service. Bring your own lights, sound system, laptop, and PowerPoint projector.) Some of these churches succeed; many fail. They usually have very well-designed websites and a strong social media presence, but with an often underpaid or unpaid pastoral staff, they struggle to stay organized. The ebb and flow of congregants means that they are often flying by the seat of their pants.

But they are attracting young people. It's too early in the movement to know how many will hang in there, but at the very least, they are turning up. And while much of evangelicalism remains fairly conservative, clashing with the surging number of Millennials who support marriage equality (nearly 70 percent, according to the PEW Research Center[5]), more liberal young evangelicals like Rob Bell and Rachel Held Evans are also beginning to have a prominent public voice. Held Evans and Bell have both written best-selling books; Bell recently announced he'd be hosting a show on Oprah Winfrey's OWN network.[6] What these Christians tap into that appeals to young religious doubters and seekers is obvious: they provide community, they emphasize a personal relationship with Jesus, and they encourage less structured and more conversational forms of prayer. Intimacy is paramount.

Where does that leave younger Catholics who are seeking the same thing? For many of them, the church can seem tone deaf when it comes to the young. World Youth Day may attract thousands of people, but many young Catholics dislike the idea of it altogether because it embodies so many of the contradictions about the church today. World Youth Day is "super conservative," one young Catholic woman told me, "and yet everyone hooks up." The Archdiocese of San Francisco in 2014 announced the opening of an outreach to young adults that features daily Latin mass, confessions, air hockey,

---

[5] "Changing Attitudes on Gay Marriage," Pew Research Center, September 24, 2014.

[6] Sarah Pulliam Bailey, "What Ever Happened to Rob Bell, the Pastor Who Questioned the Gates of Hell?" Religion News Service, December 2, 2014.

and ping pong.[7] Although I have worked with college students for fifteen years, including several stints teaching at Catholic colleges, I rarely hear them speaking Latin while playing air hockey.

The more young Catholics I spoke with, the clearer it was that priests played a huge part in their decisions about being part of the church. Acting as a kind of human filter, priests encounter the range of emotions the people I was interviewing felt about the institutional church: rage, disappointment, frustration, devotion, consolation, even love.

Many younger priests I have met are socially engaged, and they work hard to become part of the communities they serve. But I have also heard stories about and have encountered priests who are callous, cold, unfeeling, detached from the needs of their congregations. At many churches I find uninteresting homilies, a lack of warmth coming from behind the altar, and liturgical rigidity. In one of the most ethnically diverse areas in the United States, when the issue of civil rights flared in the wake of the death of multiple unarmed African American men at the hands of police late in 2014, even as protesters marched for weeks on end, I heard no mention of racism as sin, no prayers for those who had lost their lives.

Younger Catholics who care deeply about equality and justice may wonder what this silence and absence says about the state of the church. Franciscan writer Dan Horan pointed to the root of the problem in 2013: "While I know many good and humble religious and diocesan priests," he wrote, "I've encountered far too many clergy who, for whatever reason, feel they are above, better or more special than others." Horan describes these priests as "more concerned about titles, clerical attire, fancy vestments, distance between themselves and their parishioners, and focus more on what makes them distinctive than on their vocation to wash the feet of others (Jn 13:14–17), to lead with humility and to show the compassionate face of God to all."[8] Should an otherwise socially

---

[7] Brian Cahill, "The Catholic Church Is on Track to Become a Shrinking Cult," *National Catholic Reporter*, September 16, 2014.

[8] Daniel P. Horan, "Lead Us Not Into Clericalism," *America Magazine* (October 21, 2013).

engaged and compassionate person arrive at church to encounter a priest like this, what else would that person do but back away for the sake of his or her own mental health and stability?

Instead of being about priests or the hierarchy, one of the most headline-grabbing stories about Catholic youth in the last few years was the rise of a grassroots movement. When their practicing Catholic vice-principal Mark Zmuda was terminated in 2013 for legally marrying his longtime partner, Eastside Catholic High School students in Seattle staged protests outside of the archdiocesan offices, wrote letters, started Facebook and Twitter groups,[9] and, as Pope Francis encouraged Catholics to do, "made a mess."[10]

So young Catholics, like their seeker peers, are often left to their own devices when it comes to carving out a life of faith in an increasingly secular society. Like the Eastside Catholic High School students did in Seattle, they can speak up for what they want the church to be, but is anyone in the hierarchy actually listening? Michelle, who grew up in the South with her twin sister, describes her childhood as "not that Catholic." Her mother, who had been raised Lutheran, decided to convert because Catholics "wore jeans to church and she liked that better, so her decisions weren't that informed." When her family moved to a liberal-leaning city the church her parents picked was "quite a bit more conservative"

---

[9] Charlette Report, "Gay Vice Principal Mark Zmuda Files Lawsuit against Seattle Archbishop and Eastside Catholic School," *Seattle Post-Intelligencer,* March 8, 2014.

[10] This quotation is from John Thavis, "A Pope Who Likes to Shake Things Up," John Thavis blog, July 28, 2013. The official translation reads: "I want you to make yourselves heard in your dioceses, I want the noise to go out, I want the Church to go out onto the streets, I want us to resist everything worldly, everything static, everything comfortable, everything to do with clericalism, everything that might make us closed in on ourselves" ("Apostolic Journey to Rio de Janeiro on the Occasion of the XXVIII World Youth Day," Meeting with Young People from Argentina, Address of Holy Father Francis, July 25, 2013).

than any they'd previously attended. But Michelle and her sister "got into the spirituality aspect" and "took our parents along for the journey. We were diving more into theology. So we're the ones who taught them about church politics and what the priest says." It was in high school that Michelle had her first lessons in the differences among Christian denominations: "I met Bible beaters for the first time, and realized I . . . couldn't even argue about Bible passages." But her burgeoning interest in spirituality and educating herself about scripture also started to reveal a stubbornly persistent streak of wanting to define faith on her own terms. When it came to the Bible, "I guess I just tuned out the stuff I didn't agree with." That filtered into her adult life as a Catholic as well.

Michelle went to college at a Jesuit-affiliated school. She wanted to pursue theology and to go deeper into her faith life. "College was a really good progression. High school retreats were about dramatic and emotional experience. But I knew there was something deeper. I found that in Ignatian retreats and the spiritual exercises." Michelle acknowledges that, for many people, college is the time they question their religious beliefs, which she "did and didn't." But she did begin to sense a rift in the church when it came to issues of sexuality and identity. In college Michelle "got more liberal and started to realize where I disagreed with my church. I realized I'm in a closeted parish—we baptize kids of gay couples but don't talk about that. I'm not gay, and I have the luxury of not being a rock-the-boat person." But, she admits, "I started to grapple with those questions."

After college Michelle and her twin went "church shopping" for the first time. "We're very picky about our rituals and the community feeling. How present is the priest? How do they read the prayer? Do they ask you to greet your neighbor? Is the singer into it? I care about how small the church is. Does it feel intimate? That's really important." They found a church that satisfies "most of the key components," but she had a difficult time in the first months there when she felt that she "couldn't connect" and didn't have a peer group at the parish, so she joined a Bible study group at a Unitarian church and continued doing the Ignatian Spiritual Exercises at a different parish. This patching together of a religious life, she says, is reflective of the "pickiness" many people in her generation exhibit. "I think as far as spirituality is concerned, it's been harder after college to nourish myself. A lot of young adults are grappling with what they believe and why they believe it." In the Catholic churches she's attended, "I haven't met people who are willing to go in headfirst. They're tentative."

Even though she attended a Catholic college, Michelle says that she's "never hung out with a lot of religious people. Unfortunately," she admits, "the last thing I'll tell them is that I'm really spiritual. I'm afraid of getting judged. That tends to be a turnoff for friendships or otherwise. So I tend to hide it." By necessity, she says, she has "to seek out a group specifically for that purpose." She says this has also affected her dating life, because while she'd prefer a partner who's spiritual, "it's the last thing I'll tell someone I'm flirting with." When I ask if this kind of compartmentalization is socially challenging, Michelle says that "it's a bit isolating and hard. It's harder to become a good friend with me if I don't know you in a spiritual context. It's crossing that bridge into spirituality, and I'm hesitant to do it." On the other hand, "it's hard to find other people my age who are as into talking about that thing as I am. I'll meet young people at church," but when it comes to asking questions about religion and talking about it, "they're not ready to commit."

Since Michelle describes herself as "spiritually Catholic," I ask where her spirituality separates from her religious beliefs. "When the pope is in the news, my spirituality is separating from my religion. I preface conversations with 'I'm Catholic but I'm liberal, don't worry.' Ideally, they'd be one and the same." She comes back to the issue of being picky about a parish—the one she attends is experiencing a change in pastors and has had different priests coming in every week. As a result, she says, "I can't really sink into it. I'm looking for that feeling of being able to let go and be myself while being in community." She says that finding a peer group at mass isn't her primary goal, but "in spiritual interaction it takes a long time before I talk about deeply personal psychological or spiritual things with close friends. Those conversations are easier at church. Death, things people don't talk about in other circles. I'd feel closer to a church peer group than I would in other circumstances." Yet she goes out of her way to try and make connections with other young Catholics when she encounters them. "If I see someone my age I make sure to introduce myself after mass. I'm excited when someone my age shows up, and I make an effort to start a conversation."

Michelle is pursuing a graduate degree in psychology and is thinking about the connections between "how we work as humans and how that influences our spirituality." She observes that "so many people major in psychology because of natural curiosity. I think it'd be a great alternative to religion for some people. The separation isn't an either/or situation. You can have both." But she's also wary of pop psychology infiltrating religion and uses the example of "people talking about Enneagrams on retreats." She also wonders why the Catholic Church doesn't do more to teach the clergy about psychology. "If they counsel people, they should know psychology. I have a priest friend who didn't know the basic foundation of ethics with counseling. So he counseled a couple who were divorcing who were his friends. Good intentions led to awful advice. That's the first thing emphasized in counseling: boundaries."

Perhaps because Michelle is able to look at the Catholic Church both from an inside and an outside perspective through the filters of psychology, she's also aware of its confusion when it comes to her generation. "I was talking on Facebook with someone about Millennial Catholics and how we need to be welcoming and open. It's not just LGBTQ people and allies, it's the church's entire perspective on sexuality, and how it's inculturated." She says that too often the church portrays sex as "bad" and "shameful" and only a "necessity. I think that a lot of Millennials don't know this about the church—they get the 'let's not talk about it' thing. But once you take theology and realize what the church says about procreation, that's a big turnoff, even for homophobes and teenagers." For a generation that grew up with sex very much at the forefront of popular culture, the Catholic idea that it should only be procreative is deeply problematic. "Sex is a big part of Millennials' lives. To pretend it doesn't exist is probably going to ruin the church. That's a big elephant in the room."

John, who at nineteen is the youngest person I spoke with, also comes from a Catholic family, but with a difference. "My whole family comes from little Catholic towns" in the Midwest. John grew up in a town of fifty thousand people, and his parents are "fiercely apolitical." His grandparents on his father's side, how- ever, are a different story. "They're involved in LGBT equality and women's ordination and Call to Action," he says. In their living room they have a framed picture of themselves with Presi- dent Obama alongside one where they're posing with progressive Catholic hero Joan Chittister. John's grandparents loaned him a documentary about women's ordination, which he in turn loaned to his Spanish teacher in high school. She showed it to her classes at John's Catholic high school and "got into trouble" for it. When he was asked to do a project on one of his heroes, John picked Father Roy Bourgeois. "I'll never forget asking my Spanish teacher how to say female priest in Spanish, and the entire class turned around and looked at me." In his years of Catholic school John "went up against a lot of young religion teachers." He identifies more closely with Catholics of the Vatican II generation. "I love older teachers and priests."

John butted heads with the institutional Church from a young age, even while he fiercely identified as a Catholic. "I still re- member reading the 'intrinsically disordered' document [from *The Catechism of the Catholic Church*] in high school and raising a huge stink. I had gay friends, and the phrase really grated on my nerves." He had a teacher who loved John Paul II's Theology of the Body, a 1979 series of general audiences, and would often refer to it. "On the day she wanted to honor John Paul II in class, I refused to talk and put tape over my mouth."

John's grandparents "have a habit" of wearing rainbow ribbons to mass and handing out cards for the Catholic LGBTQ support organizations Dignity and Equally Blessed. John asked his grand- mother where she'd gotten the rainbow ribbon and "she had a whole spool." So John "distributed [ribbons] to thirty-five students in high school, and we all wore them to mass. I wore the rainbow ribbon through the day and was dragged into a teacher's office and lectured about promoting scandal. That's a term I get a lot. She says, 'You're not sinning but you're encouraging sin.' And she said, 'I know this is an anti-bullying thing, and you don't believe in gay marriage,' and I said, 'I do.'" For a kid growing up in the Midwest, "having grandparents who had a picture with Obama and wore rainbow ribbons was radical as hell in high school." Ironically, most of the conservative Catholic students John "rose a stink with" in Catholic school don't go to mass any more. After high school was over, "they checked out."

John went through a period of searching at the end of high school, when he wasn't sure if he identified as Catholic any more. When he arrived as a freshman at a public university, the first people to approach him were evangelicals. "I told a lot of them I was Catholic, even though I was struggling, and they left me alone." He also was approached by FOCUS—the Fellowship of Catholic University Students—which does missionary outreach on secular campuses.[11] "They reminded me of high school religion teachers fresh out of college. They love theology and John Paul II and complementarianism." John tried going to mass at the Newman Center near his college, "because I knew cute girls who went there." FOCUS again handed him a card with "all this 'how can we get in contact with you' stuff. I started to fill it out and then, thank the Lord, I forgot to finish it."

John went into college as a rhetoric major and took classes on social justice and social protest during his first semester. "I got in touch with the guy from [the local branch of] Occupy and asked who I could get in contact with for a paper." That led him to an ex-priest ("all of my favorite people are ex-priests," he adds) who lived at the local Catholic Worker house. John interviewed

---

[11] For those interested in learning more about FOCUS, see www.focus. org. For a set of highly negative accusations about FOCUS, see *Fellowship of Catholic University Students (FOCUS) Student Leader Handbook, 2008,* and comments from the source at www.wikileaks.org.

him "about a protest he'd done at an Air Force base where he'd thrown blood at planes and hit them with hammers." He also met a Catholic sister who was "the real-life version of the nun from 'Orange Is the New Black.'" As he began getting involved with leftist organizing, John understood for the first time (despite having grown up with progressive grandparents) the crossover between Catholicism and radical politics. "I found out who Dorothy Day was and who the Berrigans were. I find all these strange connections."

At this point, John says, he'd stopped going to mass. His local Newman Center "was infamous" due to the abrupt dismissal of a long-time employee by a new priest. Subsequently, "about a hundred people left the parish. They still haven't been back." John says that he "never woke up and felt, aaaaah, I should be in church. I never despaired over it or anything." Instead, he "got involved with the feminist group on campus, and they stood in as my church"; he met his girlfriend there, a women's rights advocate. "She's not religious," he admits. She's aware of his "passionate Catholic leftism. She doesn't get it, but she supports it."

The ex-priest at the Catholic Worker house invited John to a "heathen mass." The intentional eucharistic community, located in what John describes as "an old ugly office building," became his spiritual home. "There's an altar in the center," he says, and "everyone sits in a circle around the altar." At his first mass there was a sing-along to a Pete Seeger song. John describes his fellow parishioners as "very old" (later he clarifies that they're in their fifties through seventies). But in spite of the age gap, he knew something about the ad hoc, leaderless, "radical folk-mass Catholics" who had split off from the Newman Center and formed this community; it made sense to him. "All my community-organizing friends go there. Nuns go there. They're my heroes now." John is effusive when he talks about his spiritual experiences in the community. "Oh, my God, I loved it. I started to go every week. It was by choice. I felt accepted and happy there." He admits that his friends and girlfriend "didn't get it" when he invited them along, but from the beginning "it was a really cool space for me."

When I ask John whether the generation gap in his faith community ever bothers him, he says, "I've always gotten along better with older Catholics. Younger priests freak me out. The more a priest looks like me, the less I trust his theology." John recently became a double major, adding religious studies to his rhetoric major, and has been plowing through James Cone, Rosemary Radford Ruether, Margaret Farley, Mary Hunt, and other progressive theologians. He's aware that these aren't people who are taught in most seminaries. "But it's hard to be the token young person," John admits. When John is out with his college friends, "old people approach me from church. My friends call it getting 'grandsonned.'" He knows that his older Catholic friends would "like me to bring young people, but there's no focus on conversion. That's not their thing. Older people will say they'd rather die than start converting people. I really do love all of them, but all the young Catholics go to the Newman Center, and I threw my chips in with the leftists, and that's where I'll stay."

But John admits that sometimes there is a sense of absence in being the only young person around. "I have social justice friends my age who don't get the religion stuff. As much as I love getting 'grandsonned,' there's a need for young people." Trying to find a DIY workaround, instead of attempting to bring people into his faith community, John and his roommate, who "comes from the Black Protestant tradition," are starting a progressive Christian group on campus. "There are progressive Christians who go to conservative groups by default. We're starting based on some prayers we found in common. Contemplative stuff." But he admits that feeling like the lone nineteen-year-old Catholic radical can be hard. "Sometimes it really sucks. I went to the evangelical group on campus for sociological reasons. It freaked me out. There were prayer hands and flashing lights, but I thought, God damn, there's young people here. Why are they here and not where I am? But now that I'm getting into theology, I'm not going to sacrifice my identity and theology." He says that priests often ask him if he plans to return to institutional Catholicism. "If I stay here I'll go to this intentional community, but Catholic churches make me uncomfortable. I'm like, ick."

John says his intentional community is "a young community," having only been around for five or six years, and it's still figuring out what it will be. "Sometimes they'll switch out readings, and I'll bring in theology I'm reading. That's exciting. It doesn't mold you to it, it molds itself to you. I like that more than lying, which you have to do in institutional Catholic spaces." But, he admits, "the age thing does freak me out. Where are the progressive Catholics gonna be in twenty-five years? A lot of these groups are grappling with this. Okay, who are we, what are we doing? Sometimes I wish I could switch off my issues with conversion and we could pull in some young people." Perhaps this ad hoc, messy, non-institutional version of a faith life would be a challenge for others, and it can cause tension between John and his overwhelmingly secular young activist friends. "When I'm in younger social justice spaces I feel great, but sometimes it gets so bitter. I just want to be like 'Jesus will help us,' and they all freak out." So, even with the generation gap, his faith community provides the spiritual support activism doesn't. "In a lot of ways, the Catholic Left has filled that need for me. I don't have to constantly be despairing as an advocate."

Katie would also describe herself as a young Catholic activist, but she's taken John's independent version of Catholicism even further. Katie is one of the minds behind Guerrilla Communion, an ad hoc gathering of young Catholics that takes place in Katie's hometown of Washington DC. Guerrilla Communion groups recently have sprung up in Chicago and New York City as well. Katie's decision to bring Guerrilla Communion together wasn't just a way of making connections with other young Catholics; although she has a deep and meaningful connection to her Catholic identity, since she was a high school student, she's chosen not to attend mass at a church. Instead, along with her friends, she created her own version of church.

"I've always been pretty Catholic since high school, but I never had a lot of Catholic friends," Katie tells me from her living room over Skype. Like many Catholics, Katie went to a secular college. "In college, I maybe went to mass once." Part of that was being put off by what she describes as a "kooky" campus ministry. Katie knew that she was going to have to find a different way of claiming her place in the church. "For me, non-mass-going doesn't feel like a contradiction." She adds that she feels it's okay for her "not to believe some things. Catholic identity and Catholic belief aren't the same thing." And that's led to a kind of DIY understanding of religion. "My relationship with Catholicism as an adult has been on my terms and finding the pieces that worked for me."

Katie's experience of religion being self-defined is also part of why she shies away from regular churchgoing, "even while I go deeper into Catholic identity." Of her experience at a nonreligious college, she says, "I discovered a handful of Catholics" who offered different ways of thinking about an activist kind of faith. That in turn led to her first post-college job and immersion into religious life. "I wound up working with the Loretto Sisters. It was a 'nun-y' Catholicism. It was a journey of discovery." The Lorettos, long known for being boundary pushers, helped Katie to understand that Catholicism was about more than genuflecting and reciting the Creed. "The nuns do the mass gender neutral. They get arrested. That was an exciting series of discoveries." Katie worked with the Lorettos for four and a half years. Although she still speaks highly of them and says they changed her life, "at some point," when it came to the Catholic Left, "the learning curve plateaued." She adds that the Lorettos were her only real work experience until she found her current job: "I've been working for nuns since college. They're great. But it's good to have work days that aren't about processing your feelings all the time."

Guerrilla Communion was one of the ways in which Katie tried to lay claim to her religious life at the same time that she was trying to prevent activist burnout. "A spiritual home should be life-giving and not draining," she says. The idea of Guerrilla Communion emerged at a Call to Action conference, when Katie and some other young Catholics "realized we could see each other outside of conferences." That led to some brainstorming about what that might look like before they settled on the current format. "Guerrilla Communion in DC ebbs and flows in commitment and engagement," Katie says. It usually involves about fifteen people a month. She says that it "relies heavily on two or three core people who do the scheduling and grunt work."

In spite of inevitable issues of over-scheduling and stress endemic to the lives of Millennials and Gen Xers, Katie says that even if attendance isn't in blockbuster numbers, "people continue to think it's a useful part of their spiritual life." Part of what keeps the gatherings sustainable and adaptable is what she refers to as a "really simple format: potluck, introductions, icebreaker, announcements, prayer. There's sustainability in simplicity. The best Guerrilla Communion was all people who are into the same things." Her group had somebody come who was politically progressive but "by the book on teachings. After a few beers, there was a big talk on sex and masturbation. It was wild hearing somebody defend the church on this. It was cool. This is why we do this." She adds, "Where else would you have this conversation?" But it also tapped into some of Katie's growing struggles with what it means to hold a Catholic identity at the forefront of her life. That conversation, and seeing how people outside of left/ progressive Catholicism handle its contradictions up close, left Katie "with things to think about."

In addition to Katie's work with the Loretto Volunteers, she was also on the Call to Action staff for about a year and a half. When she took a new job this year with a housing nonprofit focused on issues of homelessness, balancing both of those activities "was a lot harder." In the past year, she says, "I've started to feel that maybe thinking about my faith all the time isn't the most constructive thing." She still has meaningful friendships with other young Catholics, but in her generation, "spiritual community is a little secret. You get to know people faster at a base level of trust and vulnerability." Lately, however, she's beginning to feel she may be called to something broader. The question she often asks herself these days is, "What can I do outside of the community?" An additional struggle with being part of the Catholic progressive wing is the fact that it can feel like inhabiting a place of permanent struggle. "There's so much to complain about and so much discontent," Katie admits. "That's a hard place to exist all the time."

For now, Katie is still putting together Guerrilla Communion in DC and offering advice and help to people who want to start Guerrilla Communion in other cities. But her deepest spiritual practice is a weekly centering-prayer group. It consists of just four people. "That's felt like the best thing I do. It's the simplest form of prayer that references the early Christian tradition. But it's non-hierarchical, and there's nothing to disagree with. It's just being with God and each other." As we wound up our conversation, I asked how she was planning to spend Christmas. She mentioned her Republican parents who are "progressive in religious attitudes" and her culturally Catholic mom who still attends the same parish she grew up in. "I don't go," Katie says, "but on Christmas I sing in the choir with my mom. Once a year. That's enough," she adds with a laugh.

What these young Catholics are looking for is much the same thing that any person is looking for: To be understood and known. To be seen as important, and as having important opinions. But because they pick and choose, from parishes to piecing together prayer groups to intentional communities and DIY gatherings, others might have trouble understanding that this is, in fact, a way of following a religion. However, this larger social framework must also be taken into consideration; the structures that once supported people who stay in the same religion for generations have withered away. Most Gen Xers and Millennials will have multiple jobs and even multiple careers. They are less likely to be married, or married to the same person for their entire lives, or part of a marriage that looks the way marriages once looked. They are less likely to bound by cultural or patriotic ties to one city, state, or country. They are, in short, adaptable, and they have been that way since birth. So their vision of Catholicism is also adaptable. In that way they are rather like a certain rogue, itinerant Palestinian Jew who many centuries ago created his own DIY religion. His religion moved around, brought in adherents who felt disenfranchised, and was ad hoc after his death. It looked, in other words, like a group of confused, stressed, and yet hopeful people turning to one another when the world failed to understand what they were seeking in an upper room.

Afterword

Jumping the Fence

"So," my friend said, holding onto what looked like a rotting wooden ladder, "you're going to have to climb this and then swing your leg over the top."

On an industrial block in Brooklyn, on one of the first deeply chilly nights of winter, this is how we made church: by jumping the fence. The ladder was there as assistance, as were a couple of familiar faces hovering in the dark, New York friends who'd emailed, tweeted, Facebooked, and wrangled the evening together. They'd surrounded the fence with votive candles and a Sharpie'd sign pointing the way. The pastor of this Episcopal church, who knew we were coming, had forgotten to unlock the fence, so some creativity was required. Many of the people arriving that evening were activists with some experience of creatively entering locked areas, and they'd solved the problem before we'd even arrived. My husband, who is more aware than anyone that athleticism is not among my gifts, was skeptical that I'd make it over the fence, even with a ladder as assistance, but I managed, and so did the twenty-odd people who arrived that night. We were going to make church happen, even if we might get cut or bruised in the process.

The church basement was like any other church basement, furnished with metal folding chairs and plastic folding tables, wire gridding the windows. Upstairs, the sanctuary had not so long ago been filled with food, clothing, and supplies during Hurricane Sandy, and many of the Occupy Sandy volunteers were back for this night. A Catholic sister was heating up something in the kitchen, and as we dumped jackets and scarves onto a folding table, people filtered in, bringing bags of chips, grapes, crackers, and wine. Plastic utensils were found, more people arrived: activists, writers, editors, volunteers, students, lay people, seminarians, sisters, a Jesuit brother with a backpack full of beer. No priests. We were Catholics, Nones, agnostics, seekers, and doubters. Wine went into plastic cups. There wasn't much in the way of real food, so one of the organizers called a Thai place and everyone threw dollars into a box. And while we waited, he herded everyone into a circle of chairs, and we prayed a little, in silence, and talked about religion.

I was there as a journalist, with a recorder in my pocket and a notebook on my lap, but the recording was muffled. I can decipher from my wretched handwriting some things people said. The rest is memory and the trail of stories that followed on the Internet. This was Guerrilla Communion NYC, as the sign outside let everyone know. Like its DC and Chicago manifestations, it is loosely organized around being a place where Catholics can come and talk about faith outside of a church setting. Not everyone there was Catholic, but we were all connected to the church in one way or another. So when we talked about religion, we started with the question I'd brought across the country, the one that I'd been chasing throughout fifty plus interviews, hours of research, hours of writing and revising and thinking. Where does faith begin and end for us today, in a time when institutional religion so often fails in its willingness to meet our doubts and questions?

The Catholic sister said that she thinks sometimes of being a Catholic "coach" for people who struggle with the language of faith. Others said they would look around at church and ask themselves how many people were actually listening. We talked about cultural differences and trying to stay focused on big picture issues rather than getting caught up in the superficial. The Archdiocese of New York had just announced the consolidation of 112 parishes, resulting in the closure of 31. For a few people in the room, that meant they were now "parish shopping"—a "conscious decision-making process" about what felt right and where to go that also meant an upheaval and an adjustment. Two young women described themselves as Catholics who don't go to mass—one had burned out on a bad pastor and another had actually been asked to leave a parish. "My faith isn't mass-based," she said. The other woman agreed; mass wasn't necessary for her to be Catholic. "I find faith in volunteering," she said. "And faith is brought to me by volunteering." The Jesuit brother admitted that early on he'd struggled with defining his vocation in light of things the Catholic Church did and said that he disagreed with. Ultimately, however, he felt he'd been "using an issue to hide from a calling. God is bigger than issues." Lately, he'd been drawn to more old-fashioned and ritualistic masses, even Latin masses, which he found surprising—that had never been the way he'd prayed in the past. But, for him, this became a form of surrender. "Ritual," he said, "is something bigger than you."

We ate and talked and made jokes for another hour or two before the custodian showed up, surprised to find us there, at which point we cleaned up and let ourselves out. Someone, at that point, had unlocked the fence. We said goodnight; there were hugs, a couple of people smoking, people checking their cell phones. And that was that. I flew home a few days later; they'd been chatting about planning the next meeting, and Facebook posts flickered up full of photos the next day.

Perhaps this doesn't sound like much: a bunch of people sitting around talking about faith, religion, doubt, God. Certainly, it didn't look like a church, even if it was in a church. It didn't look like a religion either: there wasn't much in the way of formal structure or a creed. When I arrived home and reassumed my occasional habit of going to mass, the rituals and creed were one way of praying, one way of grappling with faith. Conversations, throughout the year, with all of the people in this book and others—friends, spiritual directors, family, colleagues, students—were in many ways where I more often found something that felt or looked like God. The ritual remained a source of consolation when it was done well, and the Eucharist still felt like a collective embrace. But the ritual was subject to problems. When homilies were cursory and their theology thin, when the distractions of those around me became my own, when the problems of the world were neglected and prayers were self-centered, God was shallow and, ultimately, absent. When I sat and talked with people, God had depth. God was present.

This is my experience, not anyone else's. But when I line it up against the ones of the people I spoke to for this book and look at the statistics about my generation and the one after it in terms of our relationships with religion, I suspect it is not atypical. We would like to be able to be frank with one another about doubt and faith. We want to reach out to others but not to proselytize or convert. We value ritual but do not see it as inflexible and unchangeable. We are adaptable, but we honor the past. We are looking for religion to be that way as well.

Many will argue that religion should not have to change or adapt; after all, it is we who should be changed by it. The latter part is perhaps true—if religion changes us for the good. In spite of the arguments of the more hardline atheists in the media, religion stubbornly maintains the capacity to inspire compassion and love. But in an evolutionary sense, species that do not change or adapt wither and die. Many suspect that religion will go that way. Religions do sometimes behave as if they are fighting their own deaths: lashing out and condemning, becoming more and more rigid and strict. Christians believe in a resurrection, but we don't know what that will look like; for religion, there might not be a resurrection. What we see next as religion evolves could be completely surprising, unexpected, and beautiful. It could be strange, and it could be new. But religion can also fall back on kicking and fighting and grasping for control. For those who are already drifting away, that will do nothing to bring them back.

When it comes to new models for religion, those that offer me the most hope are small and community based. The New Monasticism, an ecumenical movement of loosely connected lay intentional communities, was inspired by Dietrich Bonhoeffer's idea that "the restoration of the church will surely come from a sort of new monasticism which has in common with the old only the uncompromising attitude of a life lived according to the Sermon on the Mount in the following of Christ."[1] New Monastics use grassroots techniques to build up community and are self-reliant, rather than depending on structure or higher authority. Urban-farming movements that link food production with spirituality and religion—like the lay Franciscan–run Canticle Farm in Oakland, California; The Saint Isidore Society in Denver; or San Pedro's Swedenborgian Garden Church—offer people a way to connect their desire for community with an opportunity to provide for the people around them. Young Quakers encourage people to start their own meetinghouses and even provide instructions for doing so on some of their websites.

How sustainable are these models? How long will they last? No one knows. While there is plenty of statistical evidence about why people leave organized religion behind or move away from it, there is little statistical evidence to support the longevity of these alternate models. Yet they offer the very things the people you have encountered in this book are seeking and have struggled to find, and that is why I and many others find them hopeful. It was the base communities of Catholics in Central America, for example, that kept faith alive even as the liberation theology that emerged from their faith was being oppressed.

This is not to say that larger models of religion don't matter. Plenty of remarkable people are still drawn to traditional notions of religious life. A good religious leader can guide doubters, seekers, and believers alike; these kinds of priests, pastors, rabbis, dharma teachers, and imams continue to exist, even if notions of what religion means are shifting. Their persistence to follow a vocational call in the face of difficult circumstances is evidence that institutional religion at its best still has the potential to offer us meaning. It is still able to guide us, nurture us, and provide community and consolation. But it is increasingly clear that top-down, rigid, authoritarian structures hold little appeal for generations of

---

[1] Dietrich Bonhoeffer, "Letter to Karl-Friedrich Bonhoeffer (January 14, 1935)," in *A Testament to Freedom: The Essential Writings of Dietrich Bonhoeffer*, ed. Geffrey B. Kelley, and F. Burton Nelson (New York: HarperCollins, 1990, 1995), 424.

people who were raised to be self-reliant and free-thinking. And the structural model with thousands of parishioners and one person in charge fails, in the end, to provide a deep sense of connection, of being known. When people talk about "being church," that means reaching inward, in contemplation, while simultaneously reaching outward, in service. Is that realistic without close collaborators who know and understand us? Perhaps institutional religions will become a kind of large, loose framework, and the real work of grappling with faith and doubt will happen in grassroots-based, interfaith and "inter-non-faith" cells of individuals who are drawn to one another in bonds of love and trust.

The future of faith, however, for all of our efforts to understand it, remains a mystery. But isn't faith also a mystery? And isn't that why some of us—from the students telling us on Sproul Plaza that God loves us, to the seminarians clouded with doubt but still preparing to lead congregations, to the seekers sharing a meal—still remain drawn to faith, in its many manifestations? The notion that a community of faith might be a group of people sitting around talking looks, right now, like religion. When I think back on all the people I interviewed for this book—including many I spoke to whose words do not appear here even if their influence does—what I see is a persistent desire to connect and to talk. We may talk on the Internet, or over the phone, or through the pages of a book or magazine. We may talk in church basements, on the streets, in classrooms, in living rooms. We may talk to our elders and to children at the same time. But we will talk, relentlessly, about doubt and faith and social structures, about the broken world and what we can do to repair it, about how we can be better, and what we can do to become good.